C000104255

I have been a big advocate of havi[ng] ... firms are no different. Flor sets out the ...

Running a law firm is not about just practicing law, it is running a business. Everyone expects trained lawyers to be able to deliver legal services well. It is how well they do the rest that defines who will flourish and who will not.

In a clear and readable way, Flor presents the how-to manual for achieving success. Any solicitor setting up or managing a firm who says "Na, not for me. That'll never work in my practice." will I think be making a big mistake. It is! It should be mandatory reading before leaving Blackhall Place! My only concern is that, given the title, managers running other types of service firms will not realise that they should read this book too.

    – John A. Moran, Qualified Solicitor and former Secretary General of the Department of Finance

The magic trick of a book helping lawyers market better that is actually interesting and a delight to read is one YOU must see for yourself. Flor McCarthy delivers.

    – Chris Brogan, CEO Owner Media and New York Times best-selling author

This is the ONLY manual you need to grow a successful and profitable small law firm.

    – Heather Townsend, author of 'The Go-To Expert' and 'The FT Guide to Business Networking'

This is a unique and invaluable guide to marketing and business development for solicitors. Every solicitor should read it and, more importantly, act on the ideas contained in it.

— David Rowe, Outsource

In America the solo and small firm attorney has been under attack for years. Regulations, lots of firms willing to spend large sums of money on marketing and a general public distaste for lawyers has made practice for the small firm lawyer very difficult.

For almost a decade I've lead a group of solo and small firm attorneys here in America who, despite the odds, are not only surviving but thriving.

Ireland will be no different and Flor McCarthy's book provides a roadmap to survival and success for the small firm solicitor.

— Benjamin W. Glass III, Attorney, and CEO, Great Legal Marketing

An excellent and very readable book that will inspire and stimulate ideas – an invaluable source of innovative common sense.

— Andrew Otterburn, author of 'Profitability and Law Firm Management'

I wish I had had Flor McCarthy as my mentor and guide in my law practice. His powerful book, chock full of cutting-edge tools and strategies, will transform your business and your life. If you

want to enjoy the exponential success of a deeply satisfying practice, this is a must read.

– Walt Hampton, J.D., best-selling author of 'Journeys on the Edge: Living a Life That Matters' and 'The Power Principles of Time Mastery: Do Less, Make More, Have Fun'

Flor is a trailblazer in the unstirring meadowlands that most small firm lawyers inhabit.

The legal services world is changing and there is no going back.

Any small firm lawyer who wants not only to survive but thrive in this brave new digital High Street should use Flor's book as a blueprint for their law firm.

Flor will guide you, in his effortlessly easy-on-the-eye prose, and reveal how you can look after, protect and attract new clients to your law firm by using tried and tested "in the trenches" modern marketing techniques which weren't (and still aren't) taught to you in law school.

– Paul Hajek, Solicitor and owner of Clutton Cox. Inbound and Content Marketing Expert for Law Firms

George Bernard Shaw once wrote, "The heart of an Irishman is nothing but his imagination."

Using both his heart, imagination and adding a bit of law and social media, Flor has delivered a brilliantly written book sharing real, practical and important social, business and lifestyle tips to the reader.

Want to learn how to grow your law practice while also improving the quality of your life?

Then this book is for you!

– Jon Mitchell Jackson, California Trial Lawyer of the Year (CLAY Award) | Orange County Trial Lawyer of the Year | CEO of Human.Social

Brilliant. Every law student should be given a copy and told read this and then decide whether you really want to be a solicitor. Every solicitor should read it. Brilliant does not go far enough.

– Richard Grogan, Solicitor

The Solicitor's Guide to Marketing and Growing a Business should be mandatory reading for all lawyers whether you are just starting your own law business or a seasoned lawyer. From mindset principles that are crucial to your success to proven strategies for website marketing that work, this book is full of invaluable advice. This book has the power to change the way you practice law.

– John H. Fisher, Attorney and author of 'The Power of a System'

We have only felt the first fluttering of the butterfly wings of climatic change that the legal ecosystem is about to experience. The Solicitor's Guide to Marketing and Growing a Business peppers you with many ideas, strategies and tools which should give you the confidence in this digital age and robotic era to transit from a traditional lawyer to an entrepreneurial lawyer whilst assisting you in the inevitable new role you may wish to consider in the current changing dynamics of the legal services industry.

I have no doubt that when you embrace artificial intelligence, robotics and entrepreneurism with the changing dynamics, along with the skills needed to market and rain-make in these disruptive times, which this author shares, you will indeed succeed in Turning Your Legal Practice into a Financial Success.

I wish you all every success!

– Chrissie Lightfoot – The Entrepreneur Lawyer author of 'The Naked Lawyer' and 'Tomorrow's Naked Lawyer'

This book is a practical step by step guide to marketing and enhancing your business as a solicitor. It is full of tips and useful information which can be used to get your message across.

– John Brooks, Solicitor and Chairman, Documatics

For the small to midsize law firm, legal marketing is a place of increasing bewilderment. Opportunities recognised only after they ceased to be one, money wasting possibilities in abundance, and above all the siren call of the digital sales pitchers.

Into this world without maps comes lawyer Flor McCarthy. His book fizzes with light bulb ideas. Do yourself a favour. Pick one or two, work them relentlessly, and watch your law business grow and prosper.

– Ronald E. Conway, Solicitor Advocate and author of 'Personal Injury Practice in the Sheriff Court'

In my view, it is the most practical and useful book on legal marketing/practice management that I have read. I say this for two reasons. Firstly, it is written by a practical practitioner and secondly because Flor has adopted a very generous approach of sharing his ideas/secrets with the reader. In essence the book goes beyond the theory that most books begin and end with and delves into the practical step by step approach necessary to implement the ideas set out in each chapter.

– Brendan Dillon, Solicitor

It is compelling. The platform for change of mind set delivers a strong personal message at a gallop. It feels like the author is bringing us as readers into a secret Aladdin's cave full of treasure that no one has access to. The imagery is convincing. The book is a must read for any solicitor in practice today who is serious about being in practice tomorrow.

– Augustus J. Cullen, Solicitor

Unputdownable!! An amazing compendium of knowledge and analysis to bring the legal profession kicking and screaming into the 21st Century.

Flor has successfully brought a lot of disparate thinking into a cohesive manual for the modern practitioner in a way that's accessible and, dare I say it, easy to read. "It's not about you" is the justifiable mantra – we are service providers and so we need to pitch ourselves accordingly – understand what the customer needs and tailor our services to meet them.

There's loads here for the private practice practitioner, but so much of it is relevant to the in-house lawyer where the challenge of being relevant and adding value can often be starker.

– Colm O'Connell, Solicitor and Head of Regulatory, Compliance and Dispute Resolution, Tesco Ireland

The Solicitor's Guide

to

Marketing

and

Growing a Business

How to Turn Your Legal Practice
into a Financial Success

by

Flor McCarthy

Published by

Practice Success

www.practicesuccess.ie

First Edition published in 2015

Copyright © 2015 Flor McCarthy

Printed and bound in Great Britain by

www.printandpublish.co.uk

A catalogue record for this book
is available from the British Library

ISBN 978-0-9927982-1-5

The moral right of the author has been asserted.

All rights reserved. Without limiting the rights under copyright
reserved above, no part of this publication may be reproduced,
stored in or introduced into a retrieval system, or transmitted, in
any form or by any means (electronic, mechanical, photocopying,
recording, or otherwise) without the prior written permission of
the author.

This book has been written to give you accurate and authoritative
information about the subjects it covers. You accept it with the
understanding that neither the publisher nor the author is
engaged in giving you legal or any other professional services.

For Mags, Florrie, Ernie, Blaise, Jude and Mary.

You're my why.

Acknowledgements

There are many who require special mention. My partner John along with Deirdre, Joseph, Laura and Liam at McCarthy & Co. for their assistance and encouragement throughout.

My parents Joe and Ann for everything that they have given me so selflessly both professionally and personally. I owe them both everything.

Thanks to all of those others who helped directly in the creation, completion and review of this book in one way or another: Robert Watson, Pádraig Ó Céidigh, Heather Townsend, Mitch Jackson, Chris Brogan, John Moran, Jim Daly, Paul Hajek, Ben Glass, Chrissie Lightfoot, Walt Hampton, Andrew Otterburn, Professor William Binchy, Joe Reevy, Bill Liao, Ms Justice Marie Baker, Dan Cronin, Garvan Corkery, David Rowe, Martin Lawlor, John Brooks, Kevin O'Higgins, Richard Grogan, Gus Cullen, Brendan Dillon, David Reilly, Angela Byrne, Colm O'Connell, Séamus MacGéidigh, John Fisher, Ronnie Conway and Mark Purcell.

The generosity and good nature of these people, many of whom I have never actually met, really is extraordinary and restores my faith in humanity.

Finally, thanks to Mags for her support, encouragement, sense and sound judgment and, above all, good humour; I am constantly grateful. And thanks to Florrie, Ernie, Blaise, Jude and Mary for putting up with the shoutiest Daddy in the world with his head stuck in that MacBook for far too long. All of your love, fun and companionship is what makes my life worth living.

Foreword

I always wanted to run my own business for as long as I can remember. I felt that this would give me control over my life and the direction I was taking. This would also provide me with flexibility and the opportunity to be financially independent.

However, I soon found out that it was not as simple as putting an "open for business" sign up at the front door. I felt that if I was really good at what I did, and provided a good service, then the business would look after itself. Another false assumption. Just because you are a good lawyer does not mean that you have all the necessary skills to run a law business successfully. Each role will challenge you in different ways.

So, I had to learn by trial and error. In fact, the balance of effort resulted on the error side. This is a very painful way to run a business as errors tend to be costly and, in some cases can be detrimental. I am sure that you, like me, found this to be a very lonely place. There are very few places and people you can go to for advice and direction. This can be an even greater issue when your work consists of continuously giving advice to clients.

I believe that Flor has created a unique and very important road map to help small and medium-sized law practices throughout Ireland to navigate their practice into creating success in their business. He uses common sense business strategies to challenge you to reposition your business in order to increase profitability. From a marketing perspective, Flor helps you create segmentation and focus on the 80:20 rule whereby 80% of the revenue comes from 20% of your clients. Also, as you know very well, you often spend 80% of your time satisfying 20% of your clients. This strategy alone can help you turnaround your business.

The above is but one of many fundamental examples which you can use on a practical day-to-day basis to change your business and, rather you working for your business, your business works for you.

This is one manual you can't do without, and you will refer to time and time again.

I wish you every success in business and in life.

Pádraig Ó Céidigh

Pádraig Ó Céidigh qualified as a solicitor and worked as a sole practitioner for a number of years before leaving private practice to grow Aer Arran into one of Europe's leading regional airlines. He is Adjunct Professor of Entrepreneurship and Innovation at NUI Galway and has a wide diversity of business interests.

I slept and dreamt that life was joy.

I awoke and saw that life was service.

I acted and behold, service was joy.

– Rabindranath Tagore

Contents

Introduction

The legal profession now has two very different sectors. Not the traditional split between solicitors and barristers, but rather Big Law and the rest of us. One part of the solicitors' profession comprises those large law firms who advise and represent large corporate interests and the State, and the other is made up of the types of traditional solicitors' practices up and down the country, with five partners or fewer, who represent the rest of society.

Big Law didn't have a recession; if anything it cruised right on up a gear and just started making more and more money. In recent years, the trend in Big Law in Ireland has been to get out of private client work altogether. They have far bigger and more lucrative fish to fry. As I write this 22% of the profession are employed by less than 1% of the firms representing a massive concentration of the legal manpower of the State in the firms that I refer to as Big Law Irish style. And, while law firms don't generally publish their figures, it would seem a fairly safe bet that, in true 80/20 style, the bulk of the legal fees paid in the State are concentrated within this cohort.

That's life I guess.

But it doesn't necessarily have to be this way and you don't have to accept that you just fall into the mash of the rest fighting for the scraps that Big Law leaves over, particularly when we are talking about the decent and legitimate representation of the vast majority of the plain people of Ireland; the ordinary citizens and businesses that Big Law ignores.

If you don't accept that, you have to do something about it. That's what this book is about. This book is written for you as an owner and operator of a small or medium-sized law firm, someone who is proud of what you do and damn good at it, and who makes an essential contribution to society in the process, but who knows in your heart of hearts that there has to be a better way of going about it. Presently, 92% of the Irish legal profession is made up of such law firms consisting of 5 partners or less, which for the purposes of this book I will refer to as Real Law.

Real Law is just coming out of a particularly brutal recession. Competition has become increasingly intense. We are facing seismic regulatory change. The response of many to all of this has been to just wait for things to get better. And, while economically things might be picking up, do you really want to remain at the mercy of economic cycles in the future just as you have been in the past?

The thing is you don't have to be.

This is your field manual as a Real Lawyer to developing the successful legal business you need to enable you to live the life you want no matter what the economic conditions, the competitive environment or the regulatory regime.

In order to be able to continue to serve the community in which you live and work you have to create a strong sustainable future for yourself based on a sound business model.

And the good news is you can.

Introduction

I found myself in a traditional small general practice firm when the Irish economic bubble burst and many of our practice areas evaporated along with it. But by using just the principles, techniques and systems described to you in this book, we have transformed into what is now a thriving and rapidly expanding legal business in our niche area of practice. In the process, in 2014 we won best legal website at the Irish Law Awards and I was shortlisted as a Marketer of the Year to present to over 350 lawyers from across the United States, Canada and the rest of the world at the Great Legal Marketing National Summit in Arlington, Virginia.

You can have a business that you look forward to going to work in every day, filled with clients that you enjoy working with, who recognise the value that you provide and are willing to pay for it. That isn't wishful thinking; it's a readily attainable goal that you can realistically set for yourself.

But it won't happen by continuing to do things the way that you have always done them.

To have a business filled with clients that you want to work with, first you have to identify who they are. Then, develop a business that will attract them. Finally, you will need techniques and systems that will turn them into ideal clients of your Real Law firm and keep them there. Doing all of that is exactly what we are going to concentrate on in the pages that follow.

So, if you're a Real Lawyer who wants to get back to enjoying what you do best in a profitable and sustainable legal business that you can be proud of, good, read on; I wrote this book specifically for you.

This book is written in four Parts and it is recommended that you read each in order.

- Part I gets you clear on how you need to approach all of this in your thinking – the rock you must start from.

- Part II outlines the foundations on which you can build a sustainable and profitable business.

- Part III gives you the tools you need to breathe life into your business: a steady stream of clients who need the services you provide and are able and willing to pay for them.

- Part IV tells you how to start getting it all done.

Some Terms of Reference

There are a number of terms used frequently throughout this book that may not be familiar to you as a lawyer which are defined below and referred to in capitals throughout the text:

Client Fulfilment: the services that you provide for clients in your Real Law firm.

Lead: a Prospective Client who has expressed an interest in a service that your Real Law firm provides.

Lead Conversion: the process of a converting a Lead into a client in your Real Law firm.

Lead Generation: the process of generating new Leads for your Real Law firm.

List: your list of all current and past clients of your Real Law firm along with all Prospective Clients who have identified themselves as Leads.

Prospective Client: someone with the potential to be a client but who may not have yet expressed any interest in your Real Law firm.

Real Law: the 92% of the Irish legal profession comprising small and medium law firms consisting of 5 partners or less.

Real Lawyer: a lawyer practising in Real Law who doesn't just want to own a job, but rather wants to be entrepreneurial and create a successful business.

Part I

Finding Your Solid Ground

We are in a period of constant, rapid and ever-accelerating change. It doesn't feel like we have any solid ground to work from any more. The old reliables are no longer reliable.

We can't control very much of what goes on outside of us, but the one thing we have complete control over is ourselves: how we think about the challenges we face and our attitudes towards them. That is something on which we really can depend.

So, the first thing you have to get right is the way that you think about all of this, what you should be doing, why you should do it and only then how best to go about it.

Before building a business that you'll look forward to going to work in every morning, we've got to start from solid ground.

Preferably, rock.

Chapter 1: A Buggy Whip Moment

In a time of change the learners inherit the Earth while the learned find themselves beautifully equipped to deal with a world that no longer exists.

– Eric Hoffer

Self-driving cars will soon be upon us and are likely to eliminate that thing that is a huge cause of accidents: human error. Personal injury lawyers should be worried.

Technologically, in society, we are at what I believe is a buggy whip moment.

When the automobile was first brought into general production the mass form of transportation was the horse-drawn carriage or buggy. Buggy whips were an indispensable piece of kit for any driver; manufacturers of buggy whips did very nicely indeed.

With the advent of the horseless carriage, the world of the buggy whip manufacturers changed dramatically. The internal combustion engine did not require to be whipped to go.

The pessimist might have looked upon this as a situation of doom. "Oh woe is me; my industry has been made entirely redundant by this new technology."

There are two very important aspects to this.

First of all this didn't happen overnight. There was a long transition time when buggy whip makers had plenty of time to consider the inevitable change that was facing them.

And second, how successfully one might have reacted to this change depended entirely on one's mindset in approaching the problem.

For a manufacturer who thought of the industry as just the buggy whip business the future must have looked bleak (but not entirely doomed for a reason I will return to in a moment.)

However, for manufacturers who considered themselves to be in the *driving accessory* business, on the contrary the future was full of opportunity. Suddenly there was a market for driving gloves, hats, scarves and goggles.

But even for someone who was determined not to diversify out of the production of whips there were still niches that could be exploited. Equestrian sporting enthusiasts is one example that jumps to mind as a niche market open to a manufacturer faced with the existential threat posed by this change.

And now it seems to me that we are in another buggy whip moment. Predictions are hard as the man says, particularly when they are about the future. But a relatively safe prediction is that advances in technology are inevitable and that the role of humans in many things that we consider can only be done by us (including legal work) will be reduced and in some cases eliminated entirely.

Driving is one area in which we will see big changes in the near future. This will have implications for Real Law firms, but the solution is dependent on your approach to it. For instance the overall focus of liability issues may move from negligence to defective products. Practice areas will have to respond and whole new ones may evolve.

And by all accounts we have 5 years. You can achieve almost anything in that time. But you'll achieve an awful lot more if you start right now.

So, social and technological changes from outside the profession entirely can have a profound impact on the viability and sustainability of how we do things in the little bubble that is the legal world. But even within the profession itself, the one thing that has remained consistent throughout my career has also been the ever-increasing pace of change. In truth, I think this has always been the case. I recall my father talking about his first day in the Law Society training course back in the sixties. He remembers overhearing a senior guy in the hall expressing shock and dismay at the size of the incoming class of new apprentices.

While numbers in the profession have ebbed and flowed with the recession, the long-term trend has been a rise in numbers and that seems likely to continue. But the change in the level of competition has been the least of our worries in some respects. In the years leading up to 2004 there was the fear that the PIAB would wipe out personal injury as a practice area. One practitioner standing up at a Land Registry CPD event on the electronic access service complained that we were cutting our own throats by voluntarily participating in this new system that he felt would eventually destroy conveyancing as a practice area. Whenever the court jurisdictions have changed lawyers have expected that their High Court practices would disappear.

The Legal Services Regulation Bill will bring about a real systemic change for the profession, being intended to modernise it and make it fit for purpose in the 21ˢᵗ century. Whether it achieves this purpose or merely adds further bureaucratic layers to the costs of providing legal services remains to be seen. What seems quite certain is that the change will come, for better or for worse.

In this sense legally, as well as technologically, we may also be arriving at a buggy whip moment.

As long as I've been in business, practitioners have hankered back for the good old days, when there was less competition, there was a captive market of good local profitable work in a completely uncompetitive conveyancing market and a personal injury jury trial system. The latter was long before my time, but I remember when PIAB was floated during my first few years in practice on my own, wishing it was like it had been in my father's generation and hoping that I could just get through my time in practice before the good went out of the thing altogether.

But that was the problem. Lawyers didn't drive change; they resisted it at every turn. Whenever issues were raised about indefensible aspects of the legal services market, lawyers would come out swinging with clever self-serving arguments as to why things were perfectly fine as they were or were simply too difficult to change. That entrenched, complete resistance to change led to change being imposed on us. In the case of the PIAB it also resulted in the insurance industry scoring massively to its profit at the expense of the consumer. The insurance industry succeeded in creating a Trojan horse out of the vested interests of the legal profession that everyone accepted had to be dealt with, while completely overlooking the vested interests of personal injury defendants comprising the insurance industry and the State. The big loser in all of that was the consumer and lawyers have a lot to be ashamed of in not taking the lead in driving change more constructively with a view to arriving at a fairer system.

We need to learn from those mistakes; we need to understand the need for change and get on with it. We also need to recognise that there are enormous opportunities lurking within the changes with which we are confronted, but only if we are willing to adapt. Remember, Darwinian Theory does not come to the conclusion that it is the fittest that will survive; it is those most capable of adapting to changes in their environment.

So, embrace the change.

Before getting to that, step back and think about it for a moment. There are two types of change: *external* and *internal*.

External change is what happens in the outside environment. We have very little, if any, control over this.

Changes to market conditions are not something that Real Lawyers can do anything about, and waiting around for market conditions to improve can (as we have learned from Ireland's recent recession) leave you hanging about for a very long time.

Changes to the regulatory regime are also something over which we have practically no control.

There is just no point in worrying about or railing against things over which you have no control. That's not to say that you just ignore them or pretend they're not happening; that would be insane. You've got to acknowledge and confront the reality with which you are faced, no matter how unfavourable, take whatever action you can and believe in your ability to prevail.

Internal change is another matter entirely. Internal change – change within your own business – is entirely within your control.

How you change, the pace at which you change and, importantly, when you start the change, is your work.

The thinking that caused a problem can't be expected to be any use in coming up with a solution. The first thing you have to change is your mindset and get that right. If you haven't got your head on right, it's going to be extremely difficult if not impossible to make the other changes in your practice and your life that need to flow from that.

I know that words like *mindset* sound like the type of touchy feely stuff that usually has lawyers running for the exit doors. But stick with me here, this is important.

If you're anything like I was you've come through a professional training system that is all about what you *can't* do, how things can go wrong and what is going to happen to you if (or when) they do. In your daily practice you constantly interact with other lawyers who were trained exactly the same way and who think like this too. This is not to say that all lawyers are not independent thinkers; some are. (The fact that you're reading this makes it a pretty good bet you are.) But in any group we are going to be influenced by peer pressure and won't want to leave ourselves open to ridicule by being the odd one out. And while collegiality is great and all that, we need to open our minds to new ways of thinking if we're going to be able to cope with the changes from outside that will keep coming down the tracks.

Now, I know you're an experienced and highly-trained professional, you're quite happy with your view of the world and you just want some practical things that you can do you right now in your practice to improve your performance. And there are many and I am going to tell you about them.

But, if you are going to build a sustainable business that will give you everything out of the practice of law that you want, then to do this right, before you even start on the foundations, you've got to make sure you're building on rock; and that rock is your mindset.

Insanity is to keep doing the same thing over and over again while expecting different results. If you're happy with how your practice has been performing and sure that it is perfectly situated to deal with the changes that confront you in the marketplace, then you'll do just fine without changing anything.

But if not, the changes will have to come from within.

> Your perception is key to coping with change, and change may involve as much opportunity as threat.
> The most successful are those most capable of adapting to change.
> There is no point in worrying about things you can't control.
> But you must take control of and responsibility for what you can change.
> Your mindset is the one thing over which you have complete control and you must take it.

Chapter 2: The P-Myth

We become what we think about.

– Earl Nightingale

OK, the P-Myth is a blatant play on Michael Gerber's E-Myth, a concept based around the notion of someone who is good at something, and who loves doing it, being struck by an entrepreneurial seizure and deciding to go into business doing that thing; a self-imagined entrepreneur.

But Gerber's thesis is that such people are nothing of the sort. Rather they are just doing a job in a business that they happen to own, 80% of which fail within the first 5 years and 96% fail within the first 10 years.

When it comes to the practice of law, I think most lawyers are labouring under the illusion of the P-Myth; they're professionals and if they do what they know how to do well, the business will take care of itself. "Ah but my business is different", they say. "Mine is a professional practice; that wouldn't happen in my practice." You've heard it before and, you've said it often.

But here's the news: your business is not different!

And it *is* a business. And unless you run it like that ruthlessly and relentlessly, you are just going to end up owning a job that you hate. Sound familiar?

You may have noticed that up to this point I have been referring to your *practice*. Well I am going to do something quite deliberate from this point on and refer to it as your *business*. It's a service business sure, but that's all it is; the professional practice elephant needs to leave the room. That isn't to say that there aren't particular things that apply to service businesses, in terms of regulation, the way that consumers (clients) perceive the market for our services and the way in which those services are delivered. There are, and you know these aspects of your business better than anybody out there. But it's not unique and any Real Law firm is really no different from any other business when it is broken down to its most essential components.

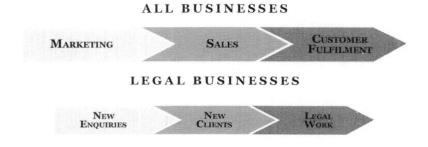

Legal Businesses are just a sub-set of all businesses.

So, from this point on, we're going to focus on your business rather than your practice. It is important to get your thinking right. The rest of the world views businesses in this way, why shouldn't you?

But of course simply changing the name of anything isn't going to make any difference on its own; and I'm not suggesting for a moment that you're so stupid that you don't see your practice as a business. The point I'm really getting to here is that the entrepreneurial seizure that Gerber describes is not something that is by any means restricted to non-legal-services businesses.

The entrepreneurial seizure grabs many lawyers too; it's how most start up in practice for themselves.

You know the story; you've probably experienced it yourself. You're working for a firm and the partners don't really recognise your contribution, and you've always wanted to be your own boss anyway. You're a pretty damn good lawyer and why waste your talent and energy doing it for somebody else when you could be running your own show.

So you take the plunge, you decide to go into practice for yourself. But the key point is that, for a great many, the focus from the start is the same: we're good lawyers, we love what we do, so why not do it for ourselves rather than somebody else.

But that is the core of the problem with this approach. We are really good at *the thing* – law. We are excellent legal technicians. The technician wants to do the work and do it really well. But a business needs more than just the technician; it needs the manager and it needs the entrepreneur. And if it neglects to fill all of these roles, it will end up being a chaotic unsatisfying job for the technician rather than a business that he or she can be proud of and that can provide the income and the lifestyle that he or she wants.

That is the real danger of the P-Myth; the idea that a great lawyer can rely solely on the practice of law for his or her business. The practice of law is just one component – a vitally important core component – but one that on its own is not going to provide a successful investment for the business owner.

This brings us to an interesting concept: up until now the only people who could own legal businesses were lawyers. But with the introduction of the Legal Services Regulation Bill that is set to change. Multi-disciplinary practices, if introduced, could mean that non-lawyers may be able to invest in legal businesses in much the same way that they can in any other area of the economy (subject to regulatory compliance of course). Were that to happen, those outside investors would apply the same principles to the running of a legal business as they might do to one in any other sector.

Currently, 30% of the personal injury market in England and Wales is handled by such firms, referred to as alternative business structures there. And they're only really getting started.

But why on Earth should you wait for some new entrant to force this change upon you if it is going to come anyway. It's not like you have to reinvent the wheel to bring any of this about; you just have to make some simple changes to the way you approach and manage your business – before someone else turns up to eat your lunch for you.

You've got one big advantage: you're the incumbent. And you've got a big head start. Why squander that? Take advantage of it.

Remember, law is *the thing* you do in your business; you need to be brilliant at doing that thing. But that's a given. That's your ticket into the game. Just being an excellent Real Lawyer is what clients expect of you in the first place. It's that basic. It's your deliverable, and it's vitally important, but it's not enough. To use a formula beloved of many legal tests: it is necessary but not sufficient.

You need more than the ability to do the basic *thing* that is the service you provide; you need a business that works for you rather than just a job that you happen to own.

➤ Think of your practice as a business.

➤ Your business is not different.

➤ Law just happens to be what you do in your business; it's your deliverable.

Chapter 3: Becoming the Expert Entrepreneur

Believe in the one who knows from experience. Trust the expert.

– Virgil

An expert entrepreneur is an oxymoron; the mindset required to be an expert is quite different from that required to be an entrepreneur.

Experts have a deep knowledge of their subject matter, they are confident and certain in that knowledge; ask an expert anything about their chosen field and they will know the answer or how to find it.

By contrast, entrepreneurs have an idea about how to do something better than it has ever been done before or indeed to do something that has never been done before. They are passionate about it and believe it can be successful; they may not know every detail of how it is going to happen but they have the drive to make it happen. They venture forth, using whatever resources they can get their hands on, learning as they go and continuously improving or innovating in a process dependent on trial and error driven by a goal.

To be a successful Real Lawyer you need to be both. As a lawyer you are already an expert at what you do. However, to be the owner of a successful business that can pay the legal expert working within it, and produce a profit, you will need to become an entrepreneur. You need to be conscious of these two roles – law and *business* – in your firm and apply appropriate thinking to each. Most importantly you must not let your craving for certainty as an expert lawyer hold you back from action in your role as a business entrepreneur.

When it comes to the actual *thing* that you do in your business – the practice of law – you should choose to do something that you can do better than anybody else, that you are passionate about and that people are willing to pay for. You should know what this is with intense clarity and then focus on it completely. You should also know what it is not.

As an Irish solicitor practising in a particular area of specialism, the idea of you aiming to be the best at what you do is actually not unrealistic. The number of people who know your area of specialism as well as you do and have your level of experience is really quite small.

But you say, "Irish solicitors are competing for a very small market of potential clients." True. But the market is not homogenous and within the market there is a huge variety of people with all different sorts of problems seeking all kinds of solutions.

The problem is that Irish solicitors have in the main remained generalists, and to an uninformed consumer, generalists all look the same.

The Prospective Client does not have the knowledge to be able to choose one generalist over another, other than basing a decision on things like familiarity, convenience or price. And in truth, if all are broadly similar generalists, there may be no good reason to choose one over another other than on familiarity, convenience or price.

To stand out, the solution of course is to specialise. Hardly a new idea, I'll grant to you that. But despite the fact that it has been one of the most economically revolutionary ideas since Adam Smith's time, many Irish solicitors seem utterly determined not to use this extremely powerful economic lever.

In specialising, you can find an area in which you enjoy working, know well and can expect to be well rewarded for what you do.

When you ponder that, perhaps you immediately think of the many clients that you would disappoint by not doing all of the other things that you currently do, even if those things tend to be unproductive, unprofitable or you just hate doing them.

You think, "I'm in a small location where I can't pick and choose; I've just got to take what comes in order to keep the doors open." You don't; that is just the way that most solicitors have always done things.

It is extremely uncomfortable and counterintuitive to turn away work and to narrow the field against yourself; but it is one of the most productive and liberating things that you can do.

How creatively you want to think about this is entirely up to you. You may wish to think in basic terms of legal specialism or you may think about this differently in terms of the levels of customer service you provide, how you deliver and package your services and who you target for those services.

Obvious specialisms are practice-based:

public procurement, compulsory acquisitions, agriculture, data protection, aviation leasing, estate and tax planning, fisheries or defective product litigation.

But your specialism could be client-based:

high net-worth individuals, pharmaceutical companies, regulators, high tech start-ups, family law exclusively for women or for men, the Polish community, in-house counsel or people over 55.

Or your specialism could be defined by how you deliver your service:

luxury concierge service, low-cost no-frills conveyancing service, online based service, 24/7 service, travel-to-your-home service, services that form part of an international network or one-stop-shop services closely integrated with other disciplines.

However you do it you've got to identify your *thing*, based on what it is that you can be best at, are passionate about and that you can expect to be paid well for.

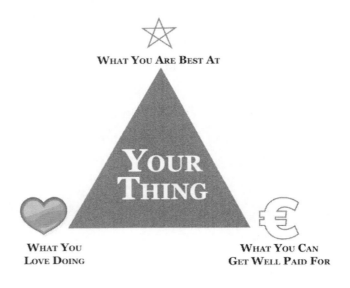

What's *Your Thing?*

Becoming the Expert Entrepreneur

Each part is vital. It's no good being brilliant at something you love that you can't make money from; you can be exceptional at something that makes you a fortune that you hate and end up miserable, or you might be able to get away with doing something highly lucrative that you love for a while but if you are no good at it or chancing your arm, you'll be found out eventually.

So far it's all about you; you've got to find something that you are best at, love and can be rewarded for, but you've also got to ensure that this is something people want. This is part of why you will be well paid for it. In marketing terms you have got to identify what you do in terms of why anyone in the market would chose you above every other alternative available in the marketplace. You've got to develop a unique selling proposition, a USP.

You may not think that what you do is unique or can be made unique, however all this requires is some imagination. You may be unique because you are an expert, you may be the recognised go-to expert in your practice area in your neck of the woods. You may be unique because of how you deliver the service. You may be unique because of who you target for your services. Or you may be unique just because you are you; you may be the person who has developed the greatest relationship of trust with your Prospective Clients which means that they will want to choose you ahead of anyone else in the market for that reason alone.

Developing your competence and confidence in what you do, how you do it and who you do it for and identifying this clearly is vital. But all of that flows from your role as expert.

Once you have done this, you then have to grow and develop the business within which this expert will work and deliver these services as an entrepreneur. Here you won't have the skills, experience and competence that you are used to but you will still have to just do it despite the uncertainty.

And you will have to do many things to develop your Real Law firm that will involve risk and pratfalls. You cannot expect to be sure of the outcomes you can hope to achieve from what you do. You will have to be prepared to try things you have not done before and some of which might seem uncomfortable. You will have to use trial and error in testing what you do in the expectation that some of it is not going to work.

This does not mean that as a business owner you should go around like a headless chicken trying things at random. Educated guesswork is where everything starts. But you will have go from there and experiment; only the market will tell you what works. To find out you will need to take action; get moving. Test and measure everything. Do more of what works and stop doing what doesn't work. In business, momentum is the key; getting started is the hard part, you can adjust your course as you go.

Solicitors are fiduciaries. It is utterly ingrained in us that we have to safeguard the interests of our principal; to not do anything that would jeopardise their interests; to quote the oath of the medical professionals, above all to do no harm.

However, when it comes to your own business, you are the principal. And you don't have an agent who's going to do any of this on your behalf. Therefore, you've got to be prepared to experiment; to try, test and measure and to fail and to learn from those mistakes.

Because if you do, and if you keep replicating the successes and disregarding the failures, and you persevere, your success is practically assured.

➤ You need to be an expert at the work you do *in* your business but an entrepreneur at how you go to work *on* your business.

➤ Find what you are best at, love doing and can get well paid for and make that *your thing*.

➤ Identify what you do in terms of why anyone in the market would choose you above every other available alternative. Develop a unique selling proposition, your USP.

➤ Your USP can be defined in terms of what you do, who you do it for or how you do it. It can be based on personal characteristics or an existing relationship with your Prospective Clients.

➤ As entrepreneur you won't have the certainty you are used to as expert; you must experiment by trial and error, testing and measuring everything and making continuous improvements based on the results.

Chapter 4: Use the Power of Positioning

It's easier to ask forgiveness than it is to get permission.

– Grace Hopper

One of the great complaints you hear from solicitors is the extent to which many of the services that they provide have become commoditised and that Prospective Clients shop exclusively on price as a result.

But the same lawyers will often have done very little to differentiate themselves from anyone else in the marketplace; in fact they will tend to prefer the collegiality of their peer group to the harsh realities of the market.

If you do not adopt a clear position within your market, there is no reason for anyone to go to you when they are in the market for legal services. If you and all of your competitors look alike, an uninformed buyer will have very little to go on to choose a lawyer. They will either go with the one that's already known, the most convenient or the cheapest.

However, those that do carve out a strong position for themselves in the marketplace will get a disproportionate amount of the business. You'll see this every day in the Law Library. Most young barristers struggle and many give up. Yet a very small number of barristers do extraordinarily well. They have established exceptional reputations for themselves and are the ones you think about when you need somebody in that area. They have created the ultimate niches and that can be extremely lucrative.

In taking a position as a Real Lawyer you must identify clearly to the market:

- What you do.
- The unique benefits that you provide.
- Why they should chose you ahead of every available alternative (bearing in mind that just doing nothing is one).

But in doing so you must by definition be less attractive to others for whom your services are not suitable or relevant.

Therefore, the job of positioning is to attract and repel in equal measure. You've got to get off the fence, get out there and show the world what it is that you do and why you are the best person to do it for them.

This brings us back to specialism of course but it also goes far beyond this. Take the example of the Law Library above. If you're a litigator, you know the counsel you need for a particular case. And if you don't know, you know how to find out and you have a pretty good nose for assessing them; you're an expert in the area yourself.

But the Law Library is an unusual market in which a group of specialists are in a market in which the buyers are experts – solicitors like you. The wider market for legal services is completely different. The Prospective Clients don't know.

And in such a market, being good at your job is not a competitive advantage. These Prospective Clients take it for granted that you are good at your job. They wouldn't consider engaging anyone who isn't; that's a given.

Use the Power of Positioning

You need to be able to differentiate yourself in some other way that enables a person to say, "Yes, this lawyer is an expert *and* they are the best lawyer for my case."

Once you create this position for yourself the dynamic of the market changes. You are someone the buyer *chooses* to have on their side rather than someone who is just like all the others for whom the predominant differentiator is probably price.

Of course it is not enough to be an expert; you already are an expert whether you like it or not. You have to project this expert status out into the marketplace. And you have to give yourself permission to do this.

Many lawyers are reluctant to give themselves permission to identify themselves as experts until they feel that they have earned the status; got their stripes as it were.

The problem is that the awarding body for this status tends to be our peer group. You wait your turn to take your place on the pecking order. Who says so? Why should you?

One of the biggest factors governing lawyers' relationships with one another is peer pressure – it is extremely powerful generally but is particularly powerful in the legal profession. Lawyers want to be respected and accepted by their peers and, don't get me wrong, collegiality and a good relationship with colleagues is undeniably a good thing. As far as it goes.

You know yourself that one of the most effective statements that can be used to unhinge another lawyer is that they are being unreasonable or out of line by reference to generally accepted norms of professional standards. And again while this is an unreservedly good thing when it comes to the standards of professional practice, it tends to spread out into a number of other areas that are not really concerned with whether the job is being done correctly or not. Professional standards are something that we may not always be able to define, but we know them when we see them and we really notice them when they are absent.

Yet when this crosses the line from professional standards to peer pressure being used to keep others in check (consciously or unconsciously) you have to recognise it for what it is and choose to disregard it.

You must give yourself permission; don't wait for someone else to determine that you've arrived and are suddenly worthy of standing out in your field.

I remember being at a legal social event many years ago when I was relatively newly set up on my own. Another young lawyer who had just done a mail shot locally entered the room. As he did a senior colleague elbowed me and a number of others nearby to say, "Here comes the postman" to disproportionate mirth and guffaws.

The guy in question was doing a pretty good job of developing his practice by direct mail and other marketing initiatives (particularly relative to all of the rest of us who were doing precisely nothing at the time). What my senior colleague was doing was telling me (perhaps quite unconsciously) that not only was this guy getting laughed at behind his back but if I thought about doing anything like it I'd have people laughing at me behind my back too.

It wasn't a big deal by any means and was just a light-hearted throw away remark that didn't mean much to anyone but it has always stayed in my mind as typical of how lawyers naturally use peer pressure to try and keep everyone in check and knowing their place within the pecking order.

Getting on well with colleagues and having a good working relationship is undoubtedly *a good thing*, but waiting in line for peer recognition to determine how you're going to develop your business is *not*; don't do it.

So, give yourself permission to claim expert status in your marketplace and create a position for yourself that clearly demonstrates the value that you deliver. Once you do, your job in finding the clients and the work that is right for you will become an awful lot easier.

> ➢ Those with a strong, clearly identifiable position in the market get a disproportionate amount of the business.
> ➢ Position yourself as an expert to your target market; make the benefits that you provide stand out from the crowd.
> ➢ You will have to be less attractive to some to be more attractive to others.
> ➢ Give yourself permission to be an expert at what you do; don't wait for someone else to decide.

Chapter 5: The Field of Dreams Fallacy

Don't go around saying the world owes you a living. The world owes you nothing. It was here first.

– Mark Twain

Many solicitors experience an entrepreneurial seizure when they decide to hang out their shingle and set up on their own. A central feature of this is that the legal technician – the person who loves doing *the thing* and is great at it – decides that they're going to make *that thing* that they're most passionate about their business. They love it after all and are great doing it; so what could make more sense than to base their business on it.

This kind of wild-eyed optimism is best summed up by the Kevin Costner movie *The Field of Dreams*. The film involves a man's dream to build a baseball diamond in a cornfield in the middle of nowhere. It's a mad dream, but he's passionate about it and the message from the film is: build it and they will come. He does. And they do.

However, when we return from planet Hollywood, things aren't quite so rosy with this picture. *If You Build It They May Not Come.*

But you say, "Aren't you saying I've got to find something that I'm passionate about?" Yes, something that you're passionate about, that you can do better than anyone else *and* that people are willing to pay you well for. All three must be present. Passion or ability or indeed both of them together are simply not enough.

There is an immutable law of the universe that we have to contend with. It is this: no-one cares about you, or what you are passionate about, or what you are brilliant at, other than in terms of *what you can do for them.*

It is a simple yet brutal law; but it is also the key to having anything you want. In order to get what you want you must be able to provide value to others in the areas that they want.

So rather than build it in the hope that they will come, go and find out what they want first. Your task is to then build something that they will want and will be willing to pay you for. That's it really.

There is an entitlement mentality that you encounter in a depressingly large number of different areas in life. In legal professionals, the entitlement internal dialogue tends to go something like this: "I've worked hard to get where I am today. I've got a degree, a post-graduate qualification and a professional qualification. I've put in years of hard work in my chosen field. I deserve an income that is commensurate with the position that I have achieved for myself."

This type of entitlement thinking is doomed. Your position, your qualifications and your experience count for nothing in terms of what the world will be prepared to give you. You must think only in terms of the value that you can provide to others using your skills and experience.

Lawyers tend to think in terms of

- themselves
- their qualifications

- their experience
- their skills
- their level of empathy, customer service, quality of furniture in their reception; you name it.

NEWSFLASH – IT'S NOT ABOUT YOU!

Prospective Clients don't care where you went to school, college or university, they don't care how many years of combined experience you and your colleagues have, they are not interested in how cool your offices are. They only want to know whether you are the best person to help them solve their problem and precisely what you can do about that.

So, in everything that you do, think not in terms of what you do and what you need in your business; think in terms of what it is that you do that provides extraordinary value and benefit to your Prospective Clients; build your Real Law firm on that and they will come.

OK, so, what do they want? How do you find out?

Well, you need to do a bit of digging.

- Who are your top 20% most profitable clients?
- What are the top 20% most profitable cases you have handled?
- What are your top practice areas?
- What do you like doing?
- Who do you like working with?

Look the other way too: who are the bottom 20% of your clients, cases and practice areas from a profitability point of view. Identify what you don't like doing and who you don't like working with.

Look next at your time and where you spend it. Don't be surprised if a disproportionate amount of your time is spent on the bottom 20% doing things you don't enjoy with people you don't like. Now that you know, you can do something about it.

"But", you say, "*It's not about me!* Why are you telling me to look at what is profitable for me, what I like doing and who I like working with?"

Well, in terms of market research, if you have an existing business, or have worked in one, the best place you can start is with the information that you already have. The most profitable clients and cases you have had in the past are probably a good starting point in terms of what you can expect to get more of; no rocket science here. Of course, you may decide that you want to move into completely new practice areas which you perceive as more lucrative. But before rushing off doing that, take a look at what you've already got first.

Secondly, what people have been willing to pay you handsomely for in the past is a good indicator of where you have been providing value successfully.

Thirdly, while depending exclusively on satisfied clients telling others may not be enough to grow a business on its own (and it certainly won't be unless you do something about making it happen), it is a very important factor in what you will need to grow a high quality, high value practice: referrals. And if you like working with people it is a reasonable bet that they feel the same way. On the other hand, if you can't stand a particular client chances are they are unlikely to be thrilled with their experience of dealing with you, which in the worst case can lead to serious and time-consuming complaints and in the best case involves them just going around town telling everyone about their bad experience in dealing with you.

But, "Hang on a second", you say. "You can't have it every way, you can't have a practice filled with your best and favourite clients providing you with a steady stream of your most profitable and most satisfying cases; you've got to take the rough with the smooth."

Well you can and you don't necessarily have to, respectively. You can and you should have a Real Law firm filled with the clients and cases that you want. And while you can never get around doing the hard work that running a practice as a business entails, you can spend a lot more time on the smooth than the rough.

But, this won't happen naturally or just by accident. It won't happen if you just keep sticking to your knitting as you've always done by just letting the satisfied clients take care of themselves in the hope that they'll tell others.

To have a practice filled with the clients and cases that you want, you've got to build it so that they will *choose* to come.

> ➤ You need to build your business so that it attracts good clients.
> ➤ Clients are only interested in what you can do for them.
> ➤ Do not think in terms of what you do and what you need in your business; think in terms of what it is that you do that provides extraordinary value and benefit to your Prospective Clients.

➤ Analyse your existing practice and the time you spend by clients, cases and practice area.

Chapter 6: Can Solicitors Advertise and Should They?

Doing business without advertising is like winking at a girl in the dark. You know what you are doing but nobody else does.

— Steuart Henderson Britt

Advertising and the professions have always traditionally been uncomfortable bedfellows. This derives from some archaic notion about professionalism. I am not for a moment suggesting that the concept of professionalism in its true sense is in any way archaic. True professionalism is what we are all about; something we should live up to and be proud of. But there was an notion of some kind of gentleman professional, to whom the exigencies of commercial life did not apply. The public just somehow knew in their hearts who to call when they needed help.

And the unreformed legal services market was not very far from this up until not very long ago. The Dáil debates surrounding the passing of the Solicitors Act 2002 which led to the Solicitors Advertising Regulations 2002 provide some very eye-opening reading in terms of the attitudes held by the politicians of the day as to how solicitors might go about finding or attracting new business.

But leave aside the question of regulation and professional ethics in its orthodox sense for a moment and consider another ethical question:

Do you believe that you are the perfect lawyer for someone out there who needs your help?

And do you know from your own experience of cases where someone has suffered because either they didn't have the right legal advice and representation for them or they didn't have any legal advice or representation at all, and if they'd come to you first you could have prevented that?

Because if the answer to both of those questions is *yes*, do you not have a duty to inform that person that you can help them and that if they have your help they can avoid unnecessary problems?

And if the answer to that question is *yes*, how else are people that you have never met before (and who might be in precisely the predicament described above because they haven't met you before) going to know that you could help them if you don't get your message out to them?

This is an ethical question that comes before any other consideration of technical rules; the public have a right to know particularly when it comes to something as important as the legal services that ensure access to justice.

Historically, there has been extreme reticence on the part of the legal profession in Ireland to advertise. This led to a paradoxical situation where on the one hand we have a hue and cry about some kind of uncompetitive legal services market badly in need of reform and on the other hand a complete squeamishness about any kind of advertising which would be necessary in any properly functioning commercial market.

In giving an overview of the law of torts in Ireland in the second edition of their definitive work on the subject, Mr Justice

Can Solicitors Advertise and Should They?

Bryan M. E. McMahon and Professor William Binchy described the personal injury litigation scene in Ireland as follows:

Plaintiffs rarely have more than one major negligence action in a lifetime. Insurance companies fight thousands of such cases in every year. It is their business. As such it may be said that plaintiffs are risk averse. Insurance companies are not. The odds favour the insurer. It does not matter whether a particular case costs more to settle than the insurance company would actually have expected, as long as the insurance company gets its annual sums right on balance. As long as premium income exceeds liability payments and running expenses then the insurers make a profit. Variations in individual transactions have little significance for insurance companies.

The injured person, on the other hand, is only concerned with the outcome of his particular case. If his injuries are sufficiently serious, then the forensic lottery becomes a particularly hazardous game. He must obtain as much money in compensation as possible, so that he will have a reasonable income to sustain him during his continuing disability. To avoid the risk of losing his case he may have to settle for less than his injury is worth.

Insurance companies have vast expertise and experience at their disposal when it comes to handling claims. Injured persons generally have little experience of the legal process. They select their solicitor frequently for reasons other than for his litigating or negotiating expertise. Insurance companies know the strengths and weaknesses of the small group of counsel who specialise in the motor accident field. They know whom to settle with or whom to fight in court. Plaintiffs, for the most part, select their solicitor because of a personal and continuing relationship. Frequently, they do not know which lawyers specialise in the area. Moreover, they have no way of gauging the advice their lawyers give them.

While much has changed in the personal injury scene since that was written in 1990, little has changed in the way in which plaintiffs select their lawyers. And as a result, defendant insurance companies continue to have a huge advantage over uninformed plaintiffs.

In fact, to stick with this practice area of personal injuries for a moment, we now have a State agency, the Injuries Board which actively advertises encouraging the public to proceed to have their claims assessed without the benefit of any legal advice whatsoever. You know that unrepresented claimants to the Injuries Board face a raft of unfairness and complexity in terms of how the procedures are stacked against them; when we have supposedly independent government bodies advertising against the use of lawyers in this process, the public have to hear the other side of that argument. But how will they if lawyers don't speak up for themselves?

While I was writing this there was a campaign in the Gazette over a number of months which was picked up in the national press, to the effect that the Law Society were clamping down on unlawful solicitor's advertising. This is a good thing for self-respecting professionals. Those unlawful practices generally tend to be adopted either by those who have decided to take a calculated risk and simply ignore the regulations or by non-lawyers operating claims sites sometimes from outside the jurisdiction. Respectable lawyers wanting to advertise within the scope of the legislation and regulations have been competing with both hands tied behind their backs when it comes to these non-compliant operators, so the sooner they are shut down the better.

However, that is not to say that lawyers should be sheepish about advertising. The public has a right to know; Real Lawyers are entitled to, and should, robustly advertise their services in compliance with regulations in a normal functioning commercial market.

In light of all of this, there is a detailed review of the regulatory regime in Appendix 1.

> ➤ You are the perfect lawyer for someone who needs your help.
> ➤ You do have a duty to inform Prospective Clients of what you can do to help them and how they might avoid unnecessary problems.
> ➤ The public have a right to know how you can help them and in any properly functioning commercial market lawyers must robustly advertise their services in compliance with regulations.
> ➤ Familiarise yourself with the regulatory requirements reviewed in Appendix 1.

Chapter 7: The Real Business of Your Law Firm

The purpose of business is to create and keep a customer.

— Peter F. Drucker

To summarise what we've covered so far, your Real Law firm is actually a business and not some professional vocational activity. As a business it shares characteristics with businesses all over the world since the beginning of commercial time. Yes of course there are considerations that are specific to the fact that you happen to practice law in your business, but the point is that once you think of it in terms of a business, chances are it's been done before and there are lessons you can learn from that.

So ignore for now the specific deliverable in your business, *the thing* that it is that you do.

Just think in terms of all businesses generally: what do they need to operate?

Customers! In our case clients.

Of course.

But client work is only one of three main operational components necessary for a functioning business. It is very, very important. It is the core function: lawyers practise law! But all of that said it is only one component of the business and if you concentrate on this to the neglect of the others, you will have no client work to do.

So, if you're like I was when I first started out on this journey, you may get a bit confused and uncomfortable when people start talking about things like *leads* and *conversions* as essential components in the business that is your firm.

Whenever I hear the word "lead", the Jack Lemmon character in *Glengarry Glen Ross* jumps into my mind: the desperate salesman trying to close a hopeless property deal by calling people at home in the evening from a phone box in the rain. Throughout the movie the sales guys are craving the good leads; the Glengarry leads. It's an excellent but very bleak movie and it leaves you feeling kind of seedy, not really why you got into law in the first place. Surely we're not like that; we're above all that.

But, as you'll have gathered by now, your business is not different and you need to confront and accept the reality of what is involved in developing and running a successful business and just get on with it. Once you do you will find that many of the changes that you worried about as a lawyer actually present opportunities that you can exploit as an innovative business owner.

In any Real Law firm there are three main operational components: Lead Generation, Lead Conversion, and Client Fulfilment. Think of this as a funnel feeding a pipeline. The wide mouth of the funnel is the Lead Generation process. The narrow neck of the funnel is the Lead Conversion process, the pipeline is the Client Fulfilment process. Together it all forms a business development system, the whole purpose of which is to generate profits for the firm out of the end of the pipeline along with satisfied clients who will return and refer others back into the wide mouth of the funnel.

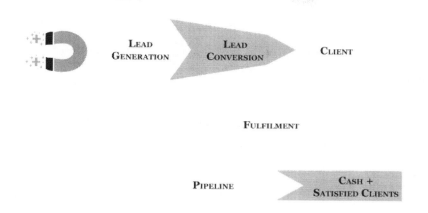

The Real Law Firm Funnel

A Lead is a Prospective Client for your Real Law firm who has expressed an interest in the services you provide.

- **Lead Generation** is the way in which you filter down the market of all the people out there in the community to those who may be interested in legal services, to those who may be interested in legal services in your practice area or your local area, to those who may be interested in the specific legal services delivered by your Real Law firm.

- **Lead Conversion** is the way in which you take someone who has expressed an interest in what you do and convert them into a client who has agreed to pay you money in return for your services.

- **Client Fulfilment** is the legal work you do for a client after they have agreed to become a client.

These three components are broadly what business people call marketing, sales and customer fulfilment respectively.

In legal colloquial parlance they are probably the functions that were divided in the practice between the finder, the minder and the grinder. Except of course that while many people have heard lip service paid to the idea of finders, minders and grinders and know that for each category of lawyer the other less palatable tasks have to be undertaken by someone (preferably someone else) very few do anything practical about it in an organised manner.

Because finders like to find, minders like to mind and grinders like to, well, grind. But no-one wants to work outside their comfort zone and very few individuals have all three attributes in the right measure. Yet fewer businesses have the required distribution of these three types of individuals.

In fact, this reliance on individuals who are seen as finders or rain makers as the way in which business development efforts are pursued in many firms is utterly depressing.

The concepts here are nothing new; and you are not so stupid as not to realise that your practice is a business and that you need clients in order to have work to do. I get that. But bear with me.

Firms have always emphasised the importance of bringing in new business to fee earners. I'm sure you can recall meetings as a young apprentice or trainee where you were drilled on how you needed to bring in business, meetings in which your shoelaces became such infinitely fascinating and captivating worlds of wonder that you couldn't take your eyes off them for the entire time. Because while there was pressure, there was no system whatsoever. How on Earth was a poor unsuspecting fee earner supposed to just "find new work".

Those types of business development meetings always had me feeling like Jack Lemmon in that phone box in the rain desperately trying to chase new business. There was nothing to work with, nothing you could control that could reasonably be expected to influence the outcome you desired on a consistent basis. It was an endless source of stress and wasted energy.

So, that kind of business development mindset is just plain daft and utterly counterproductive.

Because how on Earth can you realistically expect anyone to generate business in this way: sure networking can be very effective but only if done consistently and in a targeted way over time. You can't expect to just show up at a Chamber breakfast and come away with business. In romance and in business there is no worse aftershave than *Desperation*; the guy who is out there visibly hunting for work is often the least likely to find it for that very reason. Are your fee earners given this kind of unrealistic burden of having to go out there and *bring in business*?

Of course business development should be part and parcel of every fee earner's role; it should be part and parcel of every fee earner's day. But not as some doomed expectation to just whistle up new instructions from the rugby club. Instead it should be a business development system that forms part of what they do every day. Each person needs to know the things that they can control and influence which if done correctly will give a reasonable expectation that the process will ultimately generate new business. They still have to do the work, they still have to have the responsibility for and awareness of business development, but they do it from a position of understanding and control.

So, that's why Lead Generation, Lead Conversion and Client Fulfilment are such important components and why it is important to understand how each part of the process works and to then ensure that you have each part working for you in your business.

Lead Generation

Lead Generation is simply marketing your business.

But in this sense it is marketing in a very targeted way. You need to do precisely what the term implies: generate Leads. You do not necessarily wish to sell anything to anyone, at least not yet. This is important. Not everyone has a need for legal services, even fewer have a need for the services in the area you practise in and fewer again have a need for what you provide or would wish to acquire them from you immediately.

So you've got to narrow it down. The process by which you do this is called Lead Generation. Effectively you are going to get people to raise their hands to say that they are interested in what you have to offer.

There are a variety of ways in which you can do this and there are specifics contained in later chapters, but the important thing to grasp here is the object of the exercise. You are not trying to sell the person anything at this stage; you are simply trying to filter their level of interest. This can be done in steps, with a person indicating a greater or more specific level of interest depending on the steps through which they go in the process.

And the important thing to understand here is that these are steps taken by the person who is interested. You are not chasing but rather *drawing them toward you*; you are merely providing information, material or offers of interest that the Prospective Client is attracted to and selects for themselves based on their interest and preferences. It is a self-selection process.

This is called *qualifying the Prospective Client*. It could include:

- determining how interested the prospect is
- what need the prospect has, and
- how able the prospect is to pay for the service in question.

The more highly qualified the Prospective Client – your Lead – the more likely you are to be successful at converting that Lead into a paying client.

Lead Conversion

Lead Conversion essentially entails the process that turns an initial enquiry, or the expression of interest that might lead to that initial enquiry, into new business. This involves converting the Prospective Client into a client. Closing the sale in other words.

Let's take a domestic conveyancing example. This is a practice area that is widely regarded as commoditised and highly competitive on price. The traditional Lead Generation and Lead Conversion process in this case is usually telescoped into one as a Prospective Client does a local search either online or otherwise or gets a recommendation pursuant to which they make a cold call on the phone for a quote. The traditional reaction to this is for the office to scramble about to find someone available to take the call, who does so on the hoof. The caller is buying a house and they simply want a quote for that service. A conversation ensues pursuant to which a quote is provided. It's usually an ad hoc event and at the end of it the caller just knows the commodity (standard house purchasing services) and a quote for a price.

In these circumstances, most sensible people will shop around for a number of quotes and, all other things being equal will go with the cheapest one. And as far as most house buyers are concerned all things are equal; it's a simple job and every firm they contact will have to undertake the same work to provide the same service. In this scenario, unless the firm is prepared to quote the lowest fee in the market, the time spent on that call is probably wasted.

Now let's take this example using a Lead Generation and Lead Conversion process. The Prospective Client does a local search and takes a look at the Real Law firm's site which contains a lot of valuable information together with the option to download a helpful guide to the process. And let's say they opt for the guide which gives them lots of exactly the type of information that they are looking for about the process, what's involved and perhaps even how to go about selecting a solicitor.

The guide is offered in exchange for contact details pursuant to which the Prospective Client then receives a series of follow-up communications sent over a set time period. The first might go three days after the initial contact and explain the likely timelines in a conveyancing transaction while providing some handy tips on how to anticipate and avoid delays to ensure they get the keys to their new home when they want them. It might also explain how the firm works with them to avoid delays and provides enhanced levels of service to do everything possible to ensure that they get in for Christmas or before the big wedding or whatever their personal deadline might be. The next piece of correspondence might go 4 days after that and explain how the firm works with them to project manage every aspect of the transaction, to make it flow smoothly, as stress free and cost effectively as possible. The next correspondence a week later again might outline the likely costs involved in the transaction, transparently and comprehensively, emphasising the benefits provided by an enhanced level of customer service and clearly demonstrating the additional value provided. It might then suggest that the Prospective Client get in touch for a specific quotation or for an initial consultation.

Can you imagine the difference between that initial conversation and the ad hoc one that normally takes place? For one thing, unless you have adopted a no-frills low-cost model, those buyers who will only ever buy on price probably won't call. But that's OK, that phone call was going to be a waste of your time anyway unless you are willing to match the lowest price in the market every time.

Now when your office receives that call following your Lead Generation process, you can have a procedure for handling that call. The person who takes that call can have a very clear plan on what they need to cover on that call. The call can pick up the conversation where the correspondence has left off, emphasising the benefits of the service you provide and outlining the costs associated with doing so with confidence. The conversation that needs to take place to convert this Lead from a Prospective Client to a client takes place as part of a well thought out and consistent series of procedures that together form a system that flows naturally and directly from Lead Generation to Lead Conversion.

So, while Lead Conversion is akin to sales, if you have done your Lead Generation properly, you may not have to do a great deal of selling. The Lead will be pre-sold to a greater or lesser extent. But you do have to convert the Lead from a Prospective Client to a client, and you need a system for doing so.

The process may have a number of steps and may involve a number of subtleties and complexities to suit the particular nature of the service involved; but it needs to systematic nevertheless.

The system you use here need not be robotic or formulaic; in fact it definitely should not be and you mustn't think about systems in this way. You're used to following processes and systems every day; that is what the practice of law involves. You add a very personal dimension to the legal system you interact with and your attention to detail and intervention at key stage ensures better outcomes from that system. But the system gives you the structure so that you're sure the job is done correctly every time.

The systems you need to develop in your business for Lead Generation and Lead Conversion are no different, and at the end of the day they should just enable people to do their jobs better and to get more consistent and reliable results.

And the results of your Lead Conversion system? Clients.

Client Fulfilment

This is the delivery of the legal service itself. And you thought that this was what you did; all that you did.

You're just a lawyer after all and it's only now towards the back end of this chapter that we're getting to talk about the practice of law at all.

But this is the key point and the reason why so many legal service business owners are frustrated.

You can be the greatest lawyer in the world but if no-one knows it, and you don't have the components in place to fill your practice with clients and cases that enable you to practise your skills, all of your professional qualifications and experience are completely wasted.

But I don't need to tell you about how to do your job as a lawyer: that's what you're expert at. Except of course to emphasise that you should have systems in your practice here too.

You may recall how risk management seemed to come out of nowhere as something we all had to have in place to get insurance in the years when the professional indemnity insurance market was particularly unstable. It seemed like an awful additional burden at the time with some dreadful form filling and box ticking to meet the minimum standards.

Proprietary risk management systems seemed like a completely disproportionate burden for our businesses and it seemed like we were just being saddled by another bureaucratic cost of keeping the doors open.

Yet the experience has shown that there are tremendous benefits to be gained from these quality assurance systems in your business, from the sanity and peace of mind they provide to file management, to giving fee earners a clear structure and providing you as the business owner with meaningful control and oversight. And where you can really experience these benefits is if you do not limit these quality systems to things like risk management and integrate them with everything else that you do in your business.

Risk management systems and practice management systems are completely complementary and consistent with the business development systems that you need in the rest of your business. The quality systems that you should have for security and sanity for risk management are also perfect for ensuring uniformity and consistency in delivering the service to the client and that is an integral part of your overall business development system.

Finally, while the three components of Lead Generation, Lead Conversion and Client Fulfilment follow one another in sequence they are not necessarily linear, they are circular. The Client Fulfilment phase involves continual opportunity for further Lead Generation and of course satisfied clients are the best form of Lead Generation tool in the repeat business and referrals that they can provide for your business.

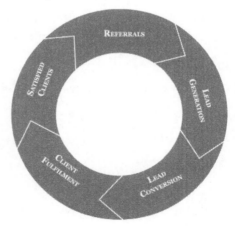

The Entire Process should be a Circular One:
Satisfied Clients return and refer new Leads

- ➤ Every business has three main operational components: Lead Generation, Lead Conversion and Client Fulfilment.
- ➤ Law is just *the thing* you do in your business; the service delivery.
- ➤ Your Lead Generation system should provide you with qualified Leads who will have pre-sold themselves.
- ➤ Your Lead Conversion system should simply continue the process of converting these Leads to clients.
- ➤ Your quality systems should ensure uniformity and consistency in delivering *the thing* that you do too – the Client Fulfilment and client care – in order to generate referrals for your business.

Chapter 8: Understanding Your Market, Your Message and Your Medium

The aim of marketing is to know and understand the customer so well the product or service fits him and sells itself.

— Peter F. Drucker

In the last chapter we discovered that your business has three main operational components: Lead Generation, which is your marketing; Lead Conversion which is your sales; and Client Fulfilment which is your service delivery.

Just as your business won't work the way it should (and it can) without all three of these components, one of them, marketing, has three fundamental elements of its own and your marketing won't work as well as it can (or at all) unless you do each of these right. They are: your market, your message and your medium.

Note that I've gone from talking about Lead Generation, to talking about marketing. Marketing is how you go about Lead Generation and this will be the major focus in the coming chapters. Done properly this can provide you with a stream of highly qualified Leads.

You have to get these elements right. But remember what we said earlier about developing your business: you don't have to have it down pat and know that it's going to work perfectly before you start. In fact you should proceed on the basis that you probably won't be right the first time and it's probably not going to work, but by trial and error (or more effectively by study, a bit of educated guesswork and help from someone who's done it before, followed by trial and error) it will work. And, if you're doing it right and you keep at it, the stuff that works will more than make up for what doesn't.

Your marketing is like a tripod; unless you have the three legs of your message, your medium and your market sound and in place, it won't support anything.

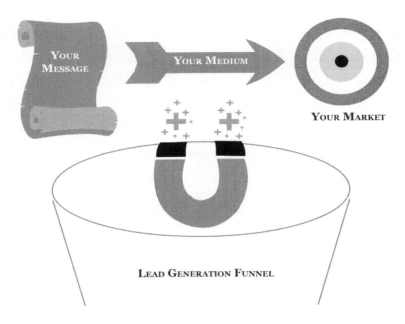

Your Marketing feeding the Mouth of Your Lead Generation Funnel breaks down into:
Your Message; Your Medium and Your Market.

Understanding Market, Message and Medium

Your Market

To begin, you must be clear on what it is that you do in your business that you are the best at, are passionate about and that people will be willing to pay you well for the value you provide as a result.

Then you need to decide on precisely who those people that you serve are going to be: you need to identify your target market. In order to fill your business with the type of clients and cases you want, you've got to identify who they are and then build the type of business to which they would be attracted.

This is where it gets uncomfortable. By identifying your target market you are by definition going to have to exclude people. Done properly you are going to have to exclude an awful lot of people. And for solicitors used to working in a traditional general practice this seems anathema.

The traditional model was to "mind" everyone in the hope that one of them is going to have a big case or a large transaction in the future and will come back to you when they do. The problem with this model is that when the person that you have been minding does have that big case or big transaction, they may not think of you at all. They simply may not be aware that you work in that area or when it comes to something very big and important to them they may want a specialist. Basing your business on blind hope that they'll come back or random chance that they'll wander in is never a good idea.

The other thing that can be uncomfortable or disheartening when it comes to doing this exercise can be the size of the market. Ireland is small and rural Ireland can be very small. It is natural to think that if you only had something with international appeal that it would sell to a mass market via the Internet, and everything would be so much easier.

Funnily enough, while it may seem counterintuitive, the opposite is often the case. As the American's say, "There's riches in niches." (Spoken in American English, these words rhyme; it doesn't quite sound the same in a Cork accent.) In other words the smaller and more focussed you can make your market, the more effective you can be as an individual or small business owner in marketing to it. Your target market will be smaller, but the people in that market will be much more receptive to your message.

Again let's take conveyancing as a simple example. At its most general it includes everything from private dwellinghouses and apartments to agricultural land to development sites and commercial property of every size and kind. Prospective Clients for conveyancing services is a target market but it's a very general one.

One obvious way in which to segment your target market is based on geography. However, if the most compelling reason that you have for anyone to use your services is your physical location, you may need to consider working on a better unique selling proposition.

The next criteria you could consider applying to your target market are demographics. Take first time buyers for example: young people and young families looking for their first home. This is a target market that is likely to be price sensitive but may have a significant long-term lifetime value for your practice if nurtured properly. Once you have identified this cohort as your target market, everything that you do to communicate with them can be tailored to suit. Your message could relate to the fact that many of them will have young kids. You might consider ads in the local school magazine or sponsoring local children's events and sporting activities that will resonate with this market.

The next way in which to further narrow the target market is by specialisation. You might wish to develop a niche here; there are any number. For example, in residential conveyancing multi-unit developments have become quite specialised since the 2011 Act and owners, purchasers, sellers and developers encountering management company issues have very specific needs in this area. Many general conveyancers find the area a pretty big headache and it's a classic example of something capable of being developed as a specialist niche.

Of these three ways in which to narrow a target market, the choice of specialism has the added benefit to the first two in that it can transcend geography or demographics. If someone has a very particular problem to which you can provide a well-defined and distinct specialist solution, Prospective Clients may be willing to travel outside their local area in order to obtain it.

The more detail you can bring to the definition of your target market for any particular service the more effective any message you are going to send to that market is going to be. Ideally, you should be able to define that market in terms of the characteristics of the individuals within it; the more detail the better.

Client Profiles

This takes the development of a niche target market to its ultimate conclusion. By now you will be comfortable with the idea of a niche and how reducing the scope of your target audience actually helps you become far more relevant and attractive to those more highly qualified prospects within that smaller group.

The idea of market segmentation is hardly a revolutionary one (at least not in the outside world, it may be relatively radical to many lawyers). You usually define a market segment by certain demographic criteria. But ideal client profiles move beyond mere demographics to consider all of the factors at play when you think about your ideal target market. In addition to demographics you think psychographics and more. Here you get into what makes them tick and what keeps them awake at night. Once you apply this and take it seriously, it can provide you with some very useful, and indeed surprising, insights into the kind of message that might reach your target market.

And there is a flip side to this. By choosing to target an ideal client, you must, by definition, exclude some other potential clients. I know, you get that: that's what niche marketing is all about. But it goes further than this. By developing a profile of the client you do *not* want, you create a clear idea of precisely the type of person you want to drive away by your marketing.

This does sound radical and uncomfortable to most, but think about it. Who is your client from hell? Picture the person. Don't tell me you don't have one.

Now the best thing you can do for yourself in your business is fire your worst clients: the 20% who are responsible for 80% of the problems, take up 80% of the time and generate less than 20% of the fees. But what if you actively drove them away in the first place, designed your marketing to actually repel them. Not only would you not have to filter them out of the Leads you get from your marketing, but they would not contact you in the first place.

Sounds scary I know, but it's really powerful. It's called *polarisation*. You develop profiles of your best client or your ideal client and your worst client or your client from hell. Then in everything that you do, you aim to speak to and attract those that would fit into the ideal profile and actively repel those that would fit into the hellish profile.

To continue with the conveyancing theme, let's look in this case at an example of an ideal client profile for commercial conveyancing:

The Ideal Client Profile

- Aged 45 to 65.
- Didn't go mad in the boom.
- Experienced, has assets and is ready to avail of opportunities.
- Has always focussed on quality in business; acquired quality property in good locations. Knows that you get what you pay for.
- Is a proper professional commercial property investor or developer.
- Appreciates the value added by a good professional in their field.
- Understands the value that a good legal operator who understands their business can bring.
- Is courteous and reasonable in their expectations. Knows what is realistic, is able to quantify risk and listens to advice.
- Is decisive and consistent.

- Is pleasant to deal with, expects the best professionally but is reasonable in demands. Knows that you will be available when needed if it's important and there's something big on but respects the fact that you have a life too.
- Knows how to let the hair down and that there's more to life than work.

The Client from Hell

- Jumped on the bandwagon in the boom. Then went spectacularly bust but is now back in the game backed by a mysteriously wealthy spouse or children.
- Thinks they're a real big shot and expects you to know it and show it.
- Treats your staff badly, is rude and aggressive and insists on always being put through to the boss immediately.
- Is unreasonably demanding with unrealistic expectations.
- Whenever there's a large transaction expects a mean bargain on fees, failing which they'll go elsewhere. Still expects the sun, moon and stars because it's a large fee regardless of what needs to be done for it. Expects lots of small stuff in the meantime for nothing.
- Is grudging and slow when it comes to paying; quick to query and argue bills.
- Is quick to find fault and apportion blame.

Understanding Market, Message and Medium

These are examples of characteristics that you might choose for each profile (at least in this example of a commercial conveyancing client). The more you can add colour to these the better. What sports or recreation do your Ideal Clients tend to like? Do they like golf, horse racing? Do they have boats or pets? Do they have young children or are they empty nesters? What are their life experiences? How do they tend to behave? What makes them tick? What about your Clients from Hell?

Create a profile for each service that you wish to promote. Then when you go to create the messages you send to your market, you can speak in very clear and direct terms with a very clear image in your mind of the individual to whom you are speaking.

You may find the exercise uncomfortable as it will be very personal. That's the whole point; for this to work you really have to get into the specifics of who you want to deal with and who you don't want to deal with in your business. Unless you've carved out a niche acting for robots, you're going to be dealing with human beings. What you're going to have to do to attract the people you want is going to be driven by every aspect of their personalities and yours.

There's a very simple reason for this; you can't be all things to all people and only a fool would try. But also, the people you want to attract are not fools and even though they may not be experts in what you do, they will have very clear ideas of what they want and what they do not want and they will base these ideas on their perceptions. How they perceive the credibility and consistency of your position in the market in terms of what it is that you do will be vital in their decision making process.

Your Message

So, you've got to identify your target market clearly before you start. Your message has to speak directly to that audience in a way that will get their attention, pique their interest, spark their desire and prompt their action.

Your message is what you put out in any of your communications. If you wish to send out a message that seeks to attract everyone and repel no-one, the message is likely to have to be so generic as to be completely ineffective. The more targeted your message is the more effective it is likely to be; it will resonate with a smaller audience but it will have much more impact on them. And in the end that smaller audience contains the only ones you would have wanted to gain business from in that area in the first place.

Think about this in plain terms: if you are selling pork sausages you are never going to have any success advertising them to vegetarians. It's going to be a monumental waste of time and money no matter how talented and creative a copywriter you are or you employ. The message in your advertising or communications has to work for your target market.

The type of advertising or marketing that you should be doing as a Real Law owner is the type that requires a direct response from the person who sees or hears it and gives that person a good reason to respond, immediately.

How do you do that? You make them an offer that they can't ignore and won't want to refuse.

Every time.

Simple as that.

Direct response marketing is the only way to travel for the Real Law firm.

While your offer should be sufficiently compelling to drive your Prospective Client to action, you mustn't allow any ambiguity on this. Your offer must include a direct call to action. This tells your Prospective Client what they must do to accept the offer: it might be to call you, to go to a web page, to leave contact details or whatever. The primary purpose of your message is to prompt action from your Prospective Client and you must state clearly what action you wish them to take.

So what kind of offer?

The offer that is most often, most suitable for marketing legal services is the offer of information. Useful and helpful information or resources that address the questions and concerns about the problems your target market are experiencing and the ways in which they might resolve them.

This type of offer is something you can really work with. Because someone who responds to this offer self-selects themselves as someone who has an interest in what it is that you are providing; they put their hands up. They are now what is referred to as a qualified Lead; they have qualified themselves as a Prospective Client for your business who you might be interested in, and have a good prospect of, doing business with.

This is called a Lead Generation offer. The beauty of it is that you can track it: you can see exactly what has worked and when. And more importantly, you can follow up with the person afterwards.

The Lead Generation offer involves an exchange: you offer helpful information or resources in exchange for contact details.

And then you use those contact details to follow up with the person in a way that is interesting, helpful and appropriate for them.

If you do this correctly, your marketing and your business will be transformed and your life will become a whole lot easier and more rewarding. We will look at the specifics of the various aspects of this in a lot more detail in subsequent chapters.

But first, let's get a very important issue out of the way: brand advertising. Brand advertising is the process of making the public aware of a particular brand and its features so that they will continue to buy it. Whenever you go to advertise anywhere or "get your message out there" in whatever way you decide, you will come across people who will speak to you about advertising in terms of your brand. When you hear these people, please smile and nod and make your excuses and as soon as you find an opportunity to do so, in a dignified fashion, run away as fast as you can.

Brand advertising does not make sense for a Real Law firm.

To be clear: branding is very important. Your brand is how you are perceived in the market. It forms part of your positioning and your reputation. However, you shouldn't be paying to advertise just to develop your brand. Your brand should come about because of what you do, how you position yourself in your marketplace and as a by-product of the direct response method of advertising described above.

Your Prospective Clients and all other sentient beings out there in the marketplace today are exposed to thousands upon thousands of brand advertisements and messages each day.

So what do they do? Well they do absolutely nothing, consciously that is; but unconsciously they just switch off. They know that they are going to be bombarded with messages that don't interest them; so their subconscious just turns on the filters, a bit like the way people don't hear a ticking clock after they've been in the same room as it for a while.

But if they're interested and it's something they want right away, it'll get their attention. If there's no immediate desire for the product or service, it may be brought to mind when it is wanted because of a branding ad they've seen at some stage. That's how big brands work. But the scale on which this is done is absolutely vast. They are thinking in terms of things like market share, where consumers can be influenced to vary their regular consumption from one product to another by brand advertising.

So, unless you have the budget of Coca Cola you really are not at the races when it comes to brand advertising and attempting to do any is like taking a bucket to the ocean; it's not likely to make much difference.

On the other hand direct response advertising provides immediate results, is completely measurable and can be scaled to suit the requirements of any Real Law firm. It is the only type of advertising you should be using and if you enhance your brand in the process that's a bonus.

Your Medium

Often the medium is the first thing anyone thinks about when it comes to marketing when in fact it should really be the last.

The reason it is often the first, is that it is usually the medium that is driving the decision to advertise to start with.

- The ad rep calls with details of a special that they are doing in your practice area that you'd be mad not to contribute to and they give you a deadline.
- A local charity or community organisation is running an event in which they'd like you to take a page in the programme and they give you a deadline.

The agenda is set by the person selling the ad space and you are just reacting. And they probably then go on to create the content for you too.

Instead, your decision making on your choice of media must be proactive and strategic rather than merely reactive and chaotic.

The media options are practically endless (subject of course to some restrictions summarised in the Regulations reviewed in Appendix 1).

The traditional medium for solicitors in Ireland before the internet was the Golden Pages. This has been in decline in recent years; and, while there may be an opportunity in experimenting with a medium that others are now ignoring, this wouldn't be where I'd start. Of course, if it's still working for you, keep doing whatever works for as long as it does.

After Golden Pages, the other traditional print media are newspapers and magazines, varying from local free sheets, through national press to specialist publications. Each have their advantages and disadvantages, with some having the capacity for some pin point accuracy once you know the market you are targeting; as always this is key.

Next there's direct mail. Yes, letters and postcards. Very few people consider this now, being of the view that everything should be online. This is a huge opportunity for you. Direct mail is one of the most powerful and under-utilised mediums out there. Don't let general ignorance of it fool you. (Interesting fact: online behemoth Google uses boring old direct mail extensively.)

Then there's TV and radio. TV is actually the first thing permitted by Regulation but it is a medium that Irish solicitors haven't gone into at all yet. Radio is much more widely utilised, particularly local stations.

And then of course there's the vast online world.

When we talk about online, we are talking about everything from your website, to your blog, your social media presence, pay-per-click advertising, banner advertising, social media advertising, mobile, email marketing and everything in between.

Online is huge and growing, just remember that like all new technology it can be used most effectively in addition to, rather than as a replacement for, the older less sexy offline tools; the best is often both, used to complement one another.

The important point is that the medium is the last thing to consider; always think first in terms of precisely who you want to reach and what you want to say to them and then decide in light of that what the best means of doing so might be.

> Your market: define your target market clearly and specifically. Narrow your focus and aim for niches.
> Develop Ideal Client profiles and Client from Hell profiles.
> Avoid brand advertising. Your message must be targeted to speak to your Ideal Client in your market and preferably drive away your Client from Hell.

➢ Your message must contain an offer that gives a good reason to respond immediately that is clearly stated as a call to action.

➢ Use the offer of useful and helpful information which you provide in exchange for the ability to follow up.

Chapter 9: Knowing Your Numbers

What is measured is managed.

– Peter Drucker

I'm a bit of a latecomer as a sports fan and while I love watching the hurling in the summer and the rugby in the winter, in truth I understand neither game very well. In fact, I am always fascinated (and a little in awe) when I hear two intelligent people who understand either game analyse it. They'll say of some aspect of a hurling match "so and so is getting cleaned out in the half back line" or they'll mention something about the "gain line" in rugby in a ruefully insightful comment, when the most I can usually muster is to start shouting!

But on whatever level you enjoy and appreciate sport, there is one thing that is pretty certain: all of the people in the stadium and many more around the country know one thing about the game – the score.

If you ask someone why they won or lost, they may say it was because of this or that but the real reason was that they didn't score as much as their competitor. It's a very straightforward and brutally honest measure.

Pádraig Ó Céidigh when developing Aer Arann said that he needed just three numbers texted to his phone each day and based on these key performance indicators (KPIs) he could tell the overall health of his business. In his case he needed to know first what the *on-time* performance was, second how many passengers they carried that day and third what percentage of the flights were full. Based on these three simple numbers he could tell whether his business was operating profitably and headed in the right direction.

In a Real Law firm the KPIs are going to vary based on the practice area but in general terms you might measure, first all new Leads generated, second new matters opened and third matters closed and cash collected.

There are two types of indicators: lead indicators and lag indicators. Lead indicators measure causes that produce effects that are measured by lag indicators.[1]

Think in terms of weight loss: the figure on the scales each week is the one we tend to notice (or that awful number on the tape around our waist) but the figures we need to focus on are the number of calories we pour down our neck each day or the amount of physical exercise we do each week. The latter are the lead indicators that will produce the results on the lag indicators of the scales and the tape. Lead here is used in a different way to "a Lead" or a Prospective Client; here I am talking about lead indicators as the leading edge of what we do that produces the results that lag behind.

The cash collected in your office account after cases close or settle is the ultimate lag indicator. It only tells you things historically. In fact most of the indicators that you will focus on in your business are lag indicators.

---

[1] The concept of lead and lag indicators is covered in The 12 Week Year by Bryan P. Moran as well as in The 4 Disciplines of Execution by Sean Covey and Chris McChesney.

Annual accounts are finalised a long time after the financial year has actually ended and are not much help in deciding the action you need to take in your business right now.

Quarterly or even monthly management accounts are better, but again even the most up-to-date and frequent information of this nature is only telling you what is going on in the rear view mirror. You need to know these things and you need to make whatever changes are required based on this information as you become aware of it; but you also have to understand their limitations.

So now you need to take the numbers back a step and look at new matters opened: good, better. But still a lag indicator; unless you depend on random chance the files only get opened because you've done something to make that happen.

OK, you measure new enquiries; better again. And you measure against these the number of letters of engagement you send out, the amount that you get back in and the numbers that actually materialise as viable new matters.

Now you have something to work with.

But you are still only measuring effects not causes; and it is here that things can get interesting.

What is driving new enquiries? Where are the Leads coming from? What can you do to generate more Leads? What actions can you and everyone in your office take to make more of what you want to happen, happen?

These are the activities that you need to measure and these are the lead indicators.

Good lead indicators include accurate measurements of traffic generation activities: overall traffic to Lead Generation pages on your website; performance of AdWords campaigns, performance of tracking and measuring on print ads; and the rate at which traffic to your website converts to new Leads. You then need to go on to measure the rate at which new Leads convert to new enquiries; the rate at which new enquiries received convert to new matters opened and the rate at which new matters opened actually close.

When you start measuring these indicators and tracking how one contributes to another, you, and everyone that works for you, can start to see exactly how what goes on in your office every day contributes to your bottom line.

Say for example you decide on a target of turnover from domestic conveyancing of €300,000 within the next eighteen months. You know that traffic landing on your conveyancing landing page generates new Leads at a rate of 20%. You know that from the time Prospective Clients opt in to your Lead Generation process to actually make an enquiry takes an average of three months and happens at a ratio of 30%. You know that the ratio at which enquiries convert to Leads following the Lead Generation process is 75%; i.e. new matters opened following the enquiry that flowed from the Lead Generation process. You know that new matters take two months on average with an average fee of €1,500.

Therefore, you will need 200 matters closing within the next eighteen months or just over 11 a month. You will need 266 new enquiries to make this happen or just over 14 a month. You will need 886 new Leads to make this happen or just over 49 a month, just under two a day. You will need 4,430 unique visitors to your landing page to make this happen or just over 246 a month, 82 a day.

It will take five months from when the first Lead is generated to the time you can expect to be paid for your first matter closed. You need to have sufficient traffic from sources driving at least 82 visitors to your landing page per day within the next month to be confident of reaching your target.

Of course all of these numbers are averages and, perhaps given the size of your market, you may not be able to produce statistically reliable data in a short space of time that will enable you to predict this with complete accuracy. But these principles and these numbers work. And as you gather the data and measure the performance of each stage of the process your ability to predict will become more and more reliable.

The type of business development meeting where you go in and start giving everyone a hard time about the amount of new business they have brought in (or more to the point, not brought in) is pretty unhelpful if you're honest. We need to recognise the practical limitations to actually going out there and whistling up new business. Some superstars are really exceptional at this; but most aren't.

However, you can have simple things that you can do every day that you know when done properly and consistently will on average lead to the number of new enquiries increasing. These will in turn lead to more letters of engagement going out which will lead to more letters of engagement coming back. This will result in an increase in the number of viable new matters being opened which will, at the end of the business cycle for the practice area that you work in, lead to the amount of cash in the bank account going up. Now you have something practical and tangible that you, and everyone else in your Real Law firm, can do at each stage in the process to develop business overall.

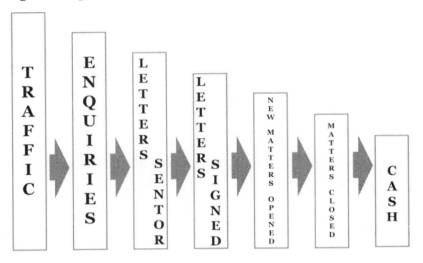

The Step by Step Progression from Traffic to Cash

And the beauty of this is that it can be measured and it can be linked to reward and suddenly everyone in the process can see the numbers; how each number influences the next one, whether they are performing and what they can expect if they do.

Now you've really got a business development system consisting of a large marketing funnel filling a pipeline of cases ultimately producing cash and satisfied clients, consistently and reliably. Next you need to ensure that you are driving sufficient traffic into the mouth of the funnel to be certain that sufficient cash will come out at the other end of the pipeline.

The ratio at which you spend cash getting traffic in at the mouth of the funnel to the rate at which you get cash out at the end of the pipeline as a direct result of that spend is your Return on Investment (ROI) and everything that you do in your business should be analysed by reference to this ROI.

The vital complementary analytical component is the period within which the return will be realised. If you can invest €1,000 that will return €2,000 in one option in two months and €1,000 that will return €5,000 in another option in six months, then the first option is much more attractive than the second. With the first you invest €1,000 at the start of month one, providing €2,000 at the end of month two which you reinvest at the start of month three, providing €4,000 at the end of month four which you reinvest at the start of month five, providing €8,000 at the end of month six. Option one is 60% better than option two over the same period.

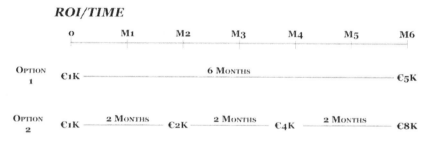

Always Think of ROI and Time

The point here is that if you understand ROI and time and you can manage cash flow effectively, a business development system based on a good marketing funnel is a money machine that can provide a return unlike anything you are going to be able to achieve anywhere else in the marketplace. In fact, viewed from this perspective, "marketing budgets" on their own can be a daft notion: if you have a proper system working for you a fixed budget will only limit your potential return, on the other hand, if you don't have such a system, having a budget to be spent on marketing may very well be a complete waste of money.

But how do you know where to start in the first place? What are the important things that you should be concentrating on?

For this you need another set of equally important numbers.

The first of these are 80 and 20.

Vilfredo Pareto was an Italian engineer and economist who discovered that 80% of the land in Italy was owned by 20% of the population. This distribution was shown to apply in many other areas and has become known as the Pareto Principle or the 80/20 Rule.

Without even having to do a huge amount of statistical analysis I would be willing to bet that you can prove this rule. For instance, are 20% of your clients responsible for 80% of the profits or perhaps more tellingly are (a different) 20% of your clients responsible for 80% of the problems?

The rule does not even need to follow an exact 80/20 ratio, it can be 90/10 and indeed the numbers don't even need to add up to 100; but the principle is always there: a disproportionately small number of causes result in a large number of effects.

Understanding this principle is one of the most powerful tools in productivity. Focus on the 20% that produces the 80% of the desired outcomes. And it can be leveraged even further: within that 20% there will be 20% with the same disproportionate level of effect and so on and so forth. Keep this in mind in everything that you do.

So in order to identify what you need to be focussing on in your business you really need to know what is there already before you go looking around elsewhere. You need to ask questions like:

- Who are the top 20% of your clients?
- What are the top 20% of your matters?
- What are the top 20% of your practice areas?
- Where do 80% of your fees come from?
- Where do you spend 80% of your time?
- Who are the worst 20% of your clients?
- What are the worst 20% of your matters?
- What are the worst 20% of your practice areas?
- Where do 80% of your problems and complaints come from?

And so on and so forth.

It is very important here that you answer these questions based on data; not anecdotally based on hunches or feelings. This involves a deep dive down into your practice to see what really makes it tick.

The results might surprise you and throw up issues or opportunities that you had never considered before.

While you're at it calculate the average life-time value of each of your clients and then do the same exercise for the top 20% and the bottom 20%.

Before getting into specific tactics on things that you need to work on, or whether what you are doing is driving things in the direction that you want them to go, you need to know these numbers for your Real Law firm.

Because then you can use them to really understand what you do and what you should be doing. What are you uniquely placed to do that you can do best; that you are passionate about and will get great satisfaction from doing; and that people will be willing to pay you what you expect for doing it?

Knowing your numbers is an essential prerequisite on your journey towards the answer to those questions.

Before we go from specific numbers, I need to mention a number that is the most dangerous number in your business: one; i.e. 1.

One is a scary number in any business. One client, one employee, one piece of technology, you name it. If your business depends solely on one thing, it is extremely vulnerable and you need to recognise this and have contingency measures in place in case anything were to happen to it.

There is great comfort from landing the big one; one big client with plenty of high quality repeat business. But if anything happens to that client – they have difficulties in their business, they have their head turned by somebody else, whatever it may be – you are at risk of loss of a vital revenue stream and you have very little control over this. To a large extent this was what happened to people in the boom, we became addicted to one thing: property. And it fuelled everything; when that particular tide went out an awful lot of us were shown to be swimming around naked.

> ➤ Establish the key performance indicators (KPIs) that are important in your business, measure them and know them.
> ➤ Everyone who works for you must know what they are responsible for and how they relate to the ultimate goals you are trying to achieve.

- ➤ Measure the direct return on every investment you make in your business and use this to analyse everything you spend in your business.
- ➤ Give everyone the ability to understand what they can do every day that will lead to the effects you need in your business. Measure those and share the measurements with everyone.
- ➤ Focus on the 20% that produces the 80% of desired outcomes.
- ➤ Remember that the most dangerous number in your business is one and make sure you've got contingencies in place in case anything happens to any one thing you must depend on.

Part II

Building Your Foundations

Moving on from the solid ground of Part I, there are four foundation stones which you will need in place to develop your practice:

1. Your List: of Leads is one of the most valuable assets in your Real Law firm; how you grow and nurture it is vital.

2. Your Website: is the hub of your business development system.

3. Your Follow-Up: is how you convert Leads to new business. You have got to have procedures in place for appropriate, effective and relevant follow-up and you have to use them.

4. Your Traffic: is the life blood that brings new Leads to your website, which you add to a List and with whom you then follow up in order to convert them to new business.

Chapter 10: The Value of Your List

Your diamonds are not in far distant mountains or in yonder seas; they are in your own backyard, if you but dig for them.

— Russell H. Conwell

The concept of your List is one that is very common in the wider marketing world; indeed much of what is modern marketing is based on it, certainly all direct response marketing. "The List" is a list of all past, present and Prospective Clients for a business. As you can imagine, for Real Law firms, it is an expression that is a little unusual, and perhaps even unnatural.

However, when you think about it – really think about it – your List is the most valuable asset in your business. Take away your buildings, your equipment, and your staff; even with all of that gone you can still start again if you have your List. Without it you have nothing.

However, lawyers ignore this extraordinarily valuable asset almost completely. These lawyers are also the ones who bemoan their perceived decline in client loyalty. Yet if you do nothing whatsoever to foster and nurture loyalty from your clients (read: your List) how on Earth can you expect to be entitled to any.

How you interact with people on your List will vary considerably depending on your situation and theirs; but interact with them you must or else you can be sure that someone else will.

Straight away, just by referring to your List in terms of three basic categories of past, present and Prospective Clients you can see something at work: it's called segmentation. The extent to which you can productively segment your List leverages its power considerably.

This is down to the relevance of the message that you send to the person that is receiving it. The more focussed, relevant and targeted the message is, the more effective it will be.

The obvious starting point is your database of current and past clients; these are your *Acres of Diamonds* as in the classic story of that name made famous by Russell Conwell.

Basically, the story goes that there was a farmer in Africa who heard of the vast riches being made in diamond mines so he sold his farm to go in search of them. He spent years fruitlessly prospecting, eventually went broke and threw himself in a river in despair and drowned.

One day the man he sold the farm to noticed a funny looking stone at the edge of the river. He took it back to the house and put it on the mantelpiece. A commercial traveller came to call and told the man he should get it checked out. The farmer shrugged and said that the riverbed was littered with the funny things. It turned out to be one of the largest uncut diamonds ever found on the continent.

We are always chasing what we don't have; the big one that will really make us. Most solicitors are obsessed with getting new clients; feeding the machine, when they really should be minding the clients they have: their real acres of diamonds.

Your existing List truly does have the potential to be your acres of diamonds, or at least it really doesn't make much sense to go looking elsewhere until you've first had a good look at what's right under your feet.

It can be a relatively major undertaking but one that only has to be done once and then kept up to date.

You need to spend a bit of time on planning and logistics first; if you've been in practice for any period of time you may have a substantial List and if you're not careful on how you go about tidying it up you can end up duplicating or wasting work easily. But it's not such a big deal once you do a bit of clear thinking on how to go about it and then just get stuck in. If you have practice management software, this may make the task much easier for you but if not you may be looking at an Excel file or similar to start with. Whatever you need to do, just do it.

You'll then need to clean up the List. There may be people who you have not dealt with for a long time or have moved away or have died. Obviously you will need to take some care to identify this where it has happened and be extremely sensitive to avoid causing offence to anyone who has been bereaved. You will also have to have regard to Data Protection legislation and Direct Marketing Regulations in how you may intend to use your List. There is a summary in Appendix 2.

The best way to clean up your List of past and present clients is to go through your client List or contact database of everyone that you have dealt with in the past and sort them into categories. In a typical firm you might choose categories such as: Active, Dormant, Deceased and Former.

- Active clients are those in good standing with you and you with them, for whom you are doing business currently or have worked in the recent past.

- Dormant are clients who you have not heard anything from for a long period of time. You might also use this category to describe clients whom it would not be appropriate to communicate with; perhaps you know that they are suffering from a lack of capacity, etc.

- Deceased is clear cut; given the nature of the profession you may have deceased clients' matters open for probate purposes, etc., but it would be completely inappropriate for any communication to issue in the deceased client's name.

- Former might include people for whom you have acted for in the past but who you know are no longer clients of yours and again with whom it would be inappropriate to communicate. For example, they may have transferred to another solicitor.

Having assigned these categories to your client List you can now simply remove Dormant, Deceased and Former clients, leaving your Active clients only, who can then form the basis for your List. Where you can take this is now really only limited by your imagination (and of course Data Protection and other regulatory considerations.)

For example, in our firm, when we first did this exercise we had never communicated with our List previously. For the 25th anniversary of the firm's establishment, we came up with the idea of having a draw to win an iPad as part of the celebrations.

We decided to carry out a client satisfaction survey which we combined with the offer of the draw to start our contact with the List. We included a business reply envelope with every letter which explained to clients in clear terms what we were doing.

The client satisfaction survey contained a comments section which provided the possibility of feedback and this produced a huge number of testimonials for the website.

Overall the feedback from this start was overwhelmingly positive. There was a very clear benefit for all recipients; this rejuvenation of our List then enabled us to commence more regular communication through our newsletter which includes an option to opt out in every issue.

Various figures have been bandied about from time to time on why clients cease to be your clients. One study revealed the following:

- 1% die
- 3% move away
- 5% go to a competitor recommended by a friend or family member
- 9% leave because of price
- 14% leave because of a grievance that didn't get handled correctly or quickly enough
- 68% leave because of *perceived indifference.*

Over two thirds of clients leave or decide not to go back simply out of perceived indifference. They think that the firm just doesn't care or takes them for granted, and when they don't get looked after in any way other than when they make contact to do some business, they're generally right.

However you do it, you can commence regular communication with your List in a way that is wholly appropriate and fully compliant with all legal requirements. What is vital is that you start. All it takes is a little imagination.

I mentioned segmentation earlier and the segmentation process itself can be a reason to get in contact. Take for example the area of wills; every client should have a will.

So, within your List you have in this example a number of segments that you can present with simple sound advice:

- You have people who have not made a will; they need to do one
- You have people who have made a will years ago and need to review and perhaps update their situation
- You have people whose marital situation has changed who may not be aware that while marriage revokes a will, divorce does not and may not have considered updating their will since their change in circumstances.

Straight away you can see some very simple steps you can take to segment your clients which would enable you to write a very specific message to each person that is likely to be highly relevant and potentially very helpful for them. It's a message that you can give in confidence that it is basically good advice and the right thing for them to do. It keeps you in contact with them in a meaningful way and shows that you are looking out for their interests.

We will come back to the method and benefits of nurturing your List of Active clients in Chapter 13 but before we do we need to consider your List of Prospective Clients.

While you should never neglect your List of Active clients, you should also be building a List of Prospective Clients. Not everyone needs legal services every day and unless you have a very large and well-tended List of Active clients, you are likely to need new business from people you haven't dealt with before.

This is what your efforts with your direct response website are all about: Lead Generation which is otherwise known as list building. You will have offered valuable information on a particular area that the person had some interest in and they will have provided you with their contact details in return for that information. That person is now a Lead on your List of Prospective Clients who has opted to receive correspondence from you voluntarily and with whom you should be following up appropriately.

Again you can further segment such Prospective Clients to great effect. The first and most basic segmentation will come with the type of information that the person selects. This is self-segmentation; the person's own choice determines how they are categorised within your List.

How you practically carry out this segmentation depends on the nature of the autoresponder or Contact Relationship Management (CRM) software you use. (We will look at these in more detail in Chapter 12.) The best will enable you to do most, if not all, of this automatically.

The self-segmentation process can be taken to any level of sophistication that you like. For instance, if a person requests information on selling a business, they might receive an email which includes a link to more information on structural planning for a family business in advance of a sale. If they opt for information on family businesses they could then receive another email with separate links to reports on issues by sector including say the agrifood sector which they click. Tags can be applied to the contact in your List with each option they select by clicking a link. You can immediately see that this person is not only interested in selling a business, but more specifically family controlled businesses and more specifically again family controlled businesses in the agrifood sector. This then allows you to speak to them in terms that are very specific and relevant to what they have clearly expressed an interest in.

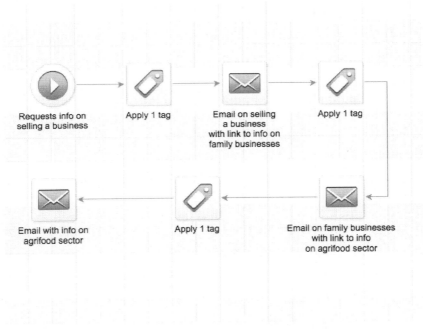

Self-segmentation in a follow up sequence

If you think in terms of your efforts to narrow the focus of your message to your target market you now have people on your List who have narrowed themselves into a niche who are much more likely to be receptive to what you have to say: they have asked for the information from you and remain open to getting it.

And your ability to convert this person from someone who is just interested to someone who wants exactly what it is that you do and is willing to pay for it increases significantly with each step in that narrowing process.

But in order to make that conversion happen you have to follow up; and that's what we'll turn to next.

> ➤ Your List is the most valuable asset in your business.
> ➤ Start your List with your Active clients and add to it with your Lead Generation activities.
> ➤ Segment your List; divide it into segments according to the interests of those in each segment. Allow people on your List to do this themselves by the information in which they express an interest.

Chapter 11: Building a Website that Works for You

...form ever follows function. This is the law.

— Louis Sullivan

Your website should be the hub of your business development system. Think of it as an online concierge service for your business by which people are directed where they need to go for the help or information that they need. But just because your website is online, do not let this limit your thinking in how you use your website. It is a very powerful tool that works best when combined with others – both online and offline.

For instance, you may use offline sources to drive traffic to your website from a print ad or other offline media source. When a visitor requests information from your website they may prefer to receive hard copies through the post in which case the follow-up sequence might go offline if that suits the visitor best.

On the other hand some visitors may come from online traffic sources via search engine traffic or pay-per-click advertising and may prefer to engage with your information and follow-up sequences via email or social media.

The important point to be clear about from the start is that while your website is a vital online presence and tool, it does not exist online in isolation and forms the control centre around which you can connect and co-ordinate all of the other parts.

Your Website Is the Hub of Your Offline and Online Traffic Generation and Follow Up Systems.

At its most basic level you need a website simply to be contactable and to confirm that you exist and are open for business. Most people will form their first impression of you from what they see online; it is your face to the world. However, it can, and it needs to be, much more than just a pretty face.

The key word in this chapter is *function*. Whatever your website, whatever type or style you like, the function that you wish your website to perform should drive every aspect of its design. Function dictates form. In architectural terms this is Bauhaus on steroids.

So the first question you must ask yourself is what function do you want your website to perform? What do you want people to do when they get there?

The point that you need to start from is to think in terms of what your Prospective Clients are likely to be looking for on the Internet, what you can deliver via your website to help them and then design the thing in the best way to do just that.

You then need to think of each page on your website as having one function and one function only: to get the visitor to take your most desired action. You need to decide what that action is for your business: to call you there and then, or to provide some contact details that will allow you to follow up with them later, etc. Whatever it may be, you need to be clear on this and then build each page around that single action.

For instance, in the domestic conveyancing Lead Generation process we used as an example in Chapter 9 we needed 49 new Leads a month to reach our target. Say for example that these Leads come from visitors to our site downloading our conveyancing guide. The single most desired action we want anyone landing on our conveyancing page to take is to download our guide in exchange for their contact details.

It is a fundamental rule of marketing that you can only ever get one response from one message. If you try to do more than this you are almost sure to fail and your message will have been wasted. Again this is counterintuitive: you think you might want to appeal to the widest possible audience and provide them with everything, but to do so will generally lead to poor performance.

However, do not confuse this with providing multiple ways to respond; this is perfectly legitimate and makes good sense. You provide one clear action to be taken but enable the visitor to take it by whatever means suits them best.

Suppose you want your website to get people to contact you about your practice area. You go to your web designer who tells you about all this stuff you've got to have and how it's all got to *look cool 'cause that's what people expect on the web now* and you've got to have a blog and you've got to have social media. Everybody's got to have social media, right?

So you get this page about the practice area. Ignore the content for a minute; we'll come to that, just think about the layout. You've got a link to your blog and all the great articles you've written, you've got your Twitter button, your Facebook button, your LinkedIn button, you've got a banner with legal news that provides links to articles from around the web on issues relevant to the practice area.

Think about this for a moment. You've paid whatever it costs you to develop a website and you've then paid whatever it costs you to get traffic to that site (and even if you think you're doing it for free by search engine optimisation it has a cost) and then, when this extraordinarily valuable visitor actually arrives at the page on the area in which you want them to be interested and to make contact with you, you give them a link that will send them off into the infinite babble of the world wide web that is Twitter, or Facebook, or LinkedIn or a news media website. When you get them to your website the last thing that you want to do is bombard them with ways to go off somewhere else.

On the other hand, let's say you bring the visitor to the same web page. It has content that is relevant and useful for them. Once they are there the only options are either to call you (with a clear button with a number), request a call back from you at your expense and at a time of their choosing, send you a message or complete a contact form or, if they are not ready to contact you directly just yet, you provide a compelling offer of further information in return for which they have to give you their contact details.

This latter page has a very clear purpose: to have the visitor contact you or provide you with their contact details before they leave the page. It provides them with multiple ways of doing so from which they can select the means that is most suitable and convenient for them. That is all.

So let's look at an example:

A firm hoping to develop probate and estate planning work from their website might develop a page which includes details of all of the many years combined experience the firm had in advising clients in this area, it might itemise the types of matters that the firms acts in including grants of probate, grants of administration, grants of administration with will annexed, de bonis non grants, administration of estates, estate planning, tax planning, contentious and non-contentious probate litigation matter and S.117 applications. It might state what specialist qualifications the firm has, for instance a solicitor with the firm may be a Trust and Estate Practitioner (TEP) registered with Society of Trust and Estate Practitioners (STEP), they might be Chartered Tax Advisers (CTA) and Associates of the Institute of Taxation in Ireland, they might have a particular interest and expertise in dealing with vulnerable clients and might be members of Solicitors for the Elderly. The page may have links to the STEP website, the Institute of Taxation website and the Solicitors for the Elderly Website along with links to other useful online legal resources like Age Action Ireland and the National Centre for the Protection for Older People.

This type of page is the exactly the type that many people, including many solicitors might conceive of when asked to create a page around probate and estate planning. More thoughtful types might realise that technical legal terms should not be used for a non-technical audience and will adapt the language describing the practice areas covered accordingly, but the gist of the content is likely to be similar.

The benefit of this content to someone looking for help online is very limited indeed; they don't know what they need. They don't know whether a grant of representation is required let alone what type might be relevant. In truth they probably don't care. They have a problem and they want to know how to solve it. The benefit of this content to the solicitor is similarly limited as the visitor is likely to leave the page without being moved to take any action towards contacting the solicitor or enquiring from them as to how they might be able to help. Indeed the links to other sites hasten and encourage this departure and in the case of links to sites like STEP, the Institute of Taxation or Solicitors for the Elderly send the visitor to sites with directories of other qualified professionals in this area.

In fact one has to question the utility of a generic practice area page of this nature in the first place as a Lead Generation tool at all.

Instead, let's focus on some of the specifics. The solicitors are clearly good at what they do. They know a lot and have a lot of experience and have put a lot of time, effort and interest into acquiring specialist knowledge and qualifications. But this in itself is not useful to someone who doesn't know what they need to solve their problem. Take for example the solicitors' interest in helping vulnerable clients. This is an area that people are worried about and may not know how or where to go about getting advice or help. Elder abuse and financial exploitation of the elderly and other vulnerable members of society is an increasing problem. Some may fear that solicitors are actually potential culprits and suspect that lawyers entrusted with money on behalf of vulnerable people may well exploit that position.

So rather than have a probate and estate planning page with all that stuff about the solicitors, what they know, what they do and how long they've been doing it, what if the solicitors had a page dedicated to explaining to a vulnerable person or a family member how they can find out if they suspect that they or their loved one is being abused or financial exploited? The page might include content that is very sensitive to the fact that it might well be another family member that is responsible and that this might lead to a source of conflict that is likely to be difficult to manage and that might seem easier to avoid than confront. The page might be based around an offer of a plain English guide to how to identify and deal with abuse of vulnerable people with lots of useful information on how to protect yourself and get help if you are being abused and how to help others if you suspect that they are.

Now when a visitor comes to this page with this problem, they are met with immediate answers and assistance. They are given a clear action to take which will give them more help and information. The guide that they download will tell them what they can do next in terms of how the solicitor may be able to help and protect them in exchange for which they will have provided their contact information.

An aspect of function is the technical platform on which your website should be built. There's no point in getting bogged down in detail on that here. Suffice to say that you should be able to control and change the content on your website easily and it should be mobile responsive, i.e. that it can be accessed from a smart phone or tablet. You'll probably have someone do all of this for you, just don't let them bamboozle you with the complexity of it all. I think the WordPress platform is best. There are many excellent commercially available themes for WordPress that make building the site itself very easy once you know what you want to have there and what you want it to do: *that's* the really important bit.

OK, so that's how to think in terms of the function your website should be designed to perform. Now let's take a look at the four different types of website a Real Law firm can use to great effect:

- A brochure website
- A direct response website
- A blog
- An e-commerce website.

Brochure Websites

A brochure site is exactly what it sounds like: a website that is effectively an online brochure. Most lawyers' websites are brochure sites.

There's nothing inherently wrong with these. A good brochure site deals with the most basic issue many people have when they go online: they're looking for someone, they may already know about them to some degree, it may be a very superficial knowledge, they may have a fragment of a name or know where they're based and they do a Google search. If the website simply confirms what the visitor needs to know and provides them with an easy way of making contact, it's done its job.

If that's all that you feel you need from a web presence, that's absolutely fine. Just make sure that it's good at fulfilling this very simple function. As mentioned in the contrasting examples described earlier, make sure that the method of contact is crystal clear and that each page on the site drives the visitor in that direction. Don't have links sending them off elsewhere.

And a word about design: design must always serve the function, the purpose the site is intended to achieve. Web designers are a fine body of men and women but the wrong web designer can kill your website; *do not* let a web designer dictate how your website should work. If the first thing that a web designer asks you about your website is how you want it to look, get another web designer. The first question they should ask is what you want your website to do. (In fact, you could use this as a simple test when vetting a web designer.)

This comes back to something that you will read again and again as you go through this book: *it's not about you.* And it's not going to be about your smart looking website either, no matter how cool the graphics, the font or the elegant and minimalist white space. The visitors to your website are only going to be interested in one thing: their problems and what you can do to help solve them. That is all.

So, a brochure site is simply what it says: an online version of the firm's brochure. It has pictures of the people and the offices; it may have funky ones, it may include a courthouse or a gavel, a pen on a parchment, a good firm handshake or some stock images of very professional looking people having a very productive meeting.

It explains how good the firm is, how much experience and expertise they have and how much they care. It says what they do, the areas they practise in, what types of conveyancing, litigation, probate, commercial work that they do (and it's probably got all of them and all of the colours in all of the sizes in all of those areas).

If that sounds familiar, do you recall creating content like that for your site? If you were anything like me the first time I did it, it was possibly one of the most excruciatingly tedious and boring tasks that you have ever done; and you were writing about you and what you did. Can you imagine what it must have been like for someone else having to actually read it? Someone who did not care about you quite as much as you did? Do you think anyone actually would read it?

In truth when I went to create our initial website in this way I did what I think everyone does: I looked around at other solicitors' websites, saw what I liked and I thought looked cool; saw what I figured I had to have: Practice Areas, About Us, Contact Page; and then proceeded to fill it with exactly the type of content that everyone else had.

But at no point did I stop to think or question whether this approach or this content was likely to be effective or had been effective in the past. I'm sure none of the others I had copied had done so either; they had just copied someone else and their web designers came up with a funky way of making it look as cool or "professional" (or both, if that is possible) as they could.

At no point did I think about the Prospective Clients and what they might want from my website, until I discovered the very simple mantra: *It's not about me*. It's about them.

Your website has to serve your business, and it must be designed exclusively to perform that function efficiently. To do that it has to be a website that people want to visit and use. You need to design it to be valuable and of service to them.

There may be nothing wrong with a brochure site on its own; that may be all you need: a simple web presence to allow people to confirm that you exist and who you are with a means of contacting you. But even then you must create the content to make it interesting and relevant to the visitor.

Direct Response Websites

A direct response site involves a rather simple progression from the brochure structure. There's a little bit more going on technically in the background, but the basic principles are merely an extension of everything covered above.

Direct response marketing is a simple concept. You design your message to engender a single, immediate, direct response to the message. You'll recall that the action desired by way of response might be to contact you with instructions on a matter: an immediate sale. Alternatively the action desired by way of response might be Lead Generation: for the visitor to raise their hand and identify themselves as someone who may be interested in this area.

Whatever the most desired action is for that page, it must be clearly stated by a call to action; the page must tell the visitor exactly what action it is you want them to take. And of course you've got to make it worth their while to do so.

The sale response in a web context is what's called "selling off the page". You have a web page with an offer for a price and the response you wish the visitor to make is to buy it straight off the page. Nice and simple.

However, for a Real Law firm selling off the page is hard, particularly when it comes to emotionally big ticket items. And notice that I'm talking about emotionally big ticket items as opposed to big *price* ticket items; there may be some overlap but they're not the same and when it comes to buying, emotions are the key factor. Choosing a lawyer is a very big ticket item emotionally.

Let's face it: very few sensible people like dealing with lawyers. Perhaps it shouldn't be that way; but it is. And the public generally distrusts lawyers, they don't understand the legal system and believe that they're going to get screwed; they have a big problem that they don't know how to solve and they're worried; they are extremely worried that if they chose the wrong lawyer they'll end up in a bigger mess than they started in; and they're worried that it may all cost them a fortune even if it's just to find out that the lawyer's no good or they don't like him or her or ... well I could go on and on.

This is what is going through your visitor's mind. So there is a huge barrier to that visitor making the decision based solely on the content of your webpage to engage you: to buy straight off, there and then.

But you say, "I don't have a sales site. There isn't a button on my page that says give me your credit card details and press buy now. I'm not selling off the page."

But isn't that first phone call the same thing? The visitor has to pluck up the courage, pick up the phone and call your office, identify themselves, give their personal information, divulge potentially extremely sensitive details about their lives and what has happened to them and all on spec to a complete stranger.

Doesn't that sound like a big deal to you emotionally? It should. That first phone call is a huge ticket item emotionally. Some people are willing to make it because they feel they just have to; but there are many who simply do not because it is too daunting.

Now, what about if that same person could come to your website and find lots of useful information about the problem that was worrying them; answers to frequently asked questions; explanations for things that have been bothering them; stuff in plain English from people that didn't seem like your typical pompous lawyers?

And what if while they were on the site there was an offer of much more information in this vein; useful stuff that could really help them understand their problem and how to go about solving it; that enters the conversation that is going on in their head? And all they have to do to get access to this information – which is likely to be more of the good quality stuff that they've already seen – is to provide their basic contact details so that the information can be sent to them immediately. That's a fair trade and does not involve anything like the intrusiveness or exposure that is involved in them getting on the phone and opening up their life to someone they've never met before.

A direct response website suits lawyers especially well for all of these reasons and it works well when it incorporates a blog (discussed shortly). The problems lawyers are trying to help people with are complex and very personal. The legal system is opaque and fraught with mistrust and suspicion to those unfamiliar with it. People often find themselves thrust into the legal world involuntarily and they would rather not be there at all.

So, you provide people in that situation with information that is targeted to them in a way that is appropriate, relevant and helpful. Once you do you are presented with an opportunity to develop a relationship with that person gradually over time through which you can earn trust. Then, when that person is ready to make contact to initiate whatever it is that they need your help with, you are the obvious (and perhaps the only) person that they are going to contact and they are going to do so having been largely convinced of your suitability for the job. In the process, they will also, if you do your job with follow-up correctly, have pre-qualified themselves sufficiently so that you know in advance that this person has a case that you can really help them with and would be willing to take on for them.

But your focus has shifted here in that if they don't want to make contact straight away – and many don't – you're now going to provide a compelling offer of *more* information. You're going to give them a reason why they might be willing to provide their contact details to you. That information could be a report, a video, an audio recording, a book; it could be all of those things. It could be emailed to them or sent to them in the post or both. But you need to have an offer; something of genuine benefit and value that your visitor is going to find interesting and useful. The delivery of that item in return for some basic contact information then becomes your most desired action. And once the visitor has taken that action, you now have an opportunity to start a relationship.

Your visitor may have left your site after they requested your information; however instead of just disappearing off into the endless chatter of the web never to think of you again, now they have gone away with something of value. And they have left something of value in return: their contact details, so that they will continue to hear from you with more of that valuable and relevant information.

Your direct response website has done its job and has generated a Lead; your job now is to follow up.

Of course, one of the means of direct response may be the same as the brochure website: the action you want the visitor to take might be to make immediate contact. In some practice areas people have an immediate pressing need and they just want to get on the phone to someone – if they do, you want to give them that option to respond.

For example if a business owner has been notified by email of an ex-parte injunction having been granted against them earlier that day ordering them to cease production immediately and they have critical orders to fill or a competitor and their solicitors show up at the front desk having just obtained an Anton Piller order and are demanding access to the premises, they just need someone on the phone immediately so make sure that they are able to get this; give them a direct number to call. (But better still have developed a relationship with them in advance by regular contact so that they don't even think of calling anyone else and the moment the crisis descends isn't their first visit to your website.)

Blogs

I mentioned a blog at the start of this section as a type of website. The word *blog* comes from weblog and in essence blogs are relatively simple websites where short articles can be published and gathered together online. For a Real Law firm a blog might comprise plain English pieces on legal topics of relevance to the firm's practice area. It is in the nature of blogs that they are updated regularly and certainly that is what the online community has come to expect. There is nothing sadder looking than a blog that hasn't had anything fresh added to it for a long time.

The fact that blogs involve fresh content being posted regularly has two main benefits: Prospective Clients visiting a blog will continually find new information; and, if the content is of good quality and continually based around the same topic, the blog may rank well for that topic in search engines.

There is a wide variety of blogging platforms out there and most, if not all, of them are free and very easy to set up. I recommend that you use WordPress for your main site and your blog, if you chose to have one, as a blog on this platform will integrate seamlessly with your main site and you will only need to be familiar with one platform in order to manage the content on your website and your blog.

For Real Law purposes, in creating and maintaining a website that others will visit and come back to, the best use of a blog is to have it form part of the main website. This way any fresh content posted on your blog is immediately refreshing your site, providing new material of interest to visitors and content that will be picked up by search engines.

And on that very point, to my mind the main function of a blog is different to the function of your website. The purpose of your blog is to generate traffic by the content that you post there. Therefore, I will return to blogs and blogging in more detail in the chapter on Traffic.

In the meantime, you should note that any posts on your blog should be geared for direct response in the same way as the rest of your site and should contain a compelling offer of something of value to the visitor together with a means of immediate response either by contacting you or requesting further information in exchange for contact details.

E-commerce Websites

An e-commerce website is where you actually sell products online and a good example is Amazon.co.uk. There are certainly opportunities where Real Law firms might use e-commerce primarily where legal services can be re-structured as products and bundled with resources telling clients how to do things for themselves. Basic document creation is the most obvious example. Irishwills.ie is an example of one e-commerce site already selling basic wills and other standard documents on a do-it-yourself basis. And the DIY aspect is a key feature of this model. This obviously poses a threat to traditional legal services providers but there is opportunity here too: most sensible people don't want to do it themselves and would be willing to pay for a premium service but only if you can show them why they should want it in the first place and the value that you deliver in providing it.

An alternative e-commerce type model to the simple sale of templates online are services like RocketLawyer.com in the US (RocketLawyer.co.uk in the UK) and LegalZoom.com. These probably pose the biggest threat to traditional law firms. Rather than simply selling products via the site, they provide membership access to documents and varying levels of support including access to a panel of lawyers on payment of a monthly fee. The RocketLawyer model works on a large scale nationwide basis in the jurisdictions in which it has operated to date and seeks to be the interface between the lawyers and the Prospective Clients, being paid by both in the process. While this is certainly a significant threat, there doesn't seem to be any reason why a cooperative of Real Law firms couldn't come together to cut out the middleman.

The prospect of the establishment of this membership site model in Ireland by third party operators seems to represent the most immediate threat to traditional independent service providers here, however with some thought and imagination there are plenty of opportunities in this too. LandlordLaw.co.uk is an example of how this has been used in the UK by an independent operator in the niche area of landlord and tenant law providing access to resources and varying degrees of support on a monthly basis. There is no reason why your Real Law firm couldn't be the innovator here.

➤ Your website should be a hub to move people from either offline or online traffic sources to whatever type of follow-up works best for them.

➤ Decide on the most desired response or action that you want your Prospective Client to take and design your site around making that happen.

➤ *It's not about you*; make your content valuable for your visitor, not all about what you do.

➤ When you get your visitor to your website do not send them off somewhere else. Remove all distractions and links to other sites; the only thing on your site other than quality content for the visitor should be ways to respond.

➤ Use your direct response site for Lead Generation. Provide information that enables the visitor to respond without having to go over the high threshold required to make contact and arrange a consultation. Use this to start a relationship to lead to that consultation.

Chapter 12: The Importance of Follow-up

Showing up is 80 percent of life.

— Woody Allen

Follow-up is the process that converts a Prospective Client into a client. It is what happens after you have generated the Lead; once someone identifies themselves as having an interest in what you do, you must follow up with them by making regular contact with a view to taking them to the next stage. Follow-up can be done in a variety of ways: by e-mail, by post, on the phone or in person. What's important is that you are keeping in regular contact with the person who has a need for and has expressed an interest in your services; you follow up with them with a view to developing that interest into actually doing business with you. In this way, follow-up is a systematic sales or Lead Conversion process.

Follow-up, and indeed sales, is a funny one for lawyers. Lawyers tend to think of selling, or the process that leads to the sale, like negotiation.

Being professional negotiators has conditioned much of lawyers' thinking. In negotiation you make your offer and wait for the other side to come back to you. Follow-up in this context can be a big no-no and can give all the wrong signals.

But sales, or the communications that might ultimately lead to sales, are not negotiations and if you take the same "hands off, one and only one contact and wait for the other side to come back to you" approach it won't work.

Not that you need to appear desperate or weak in the process; these impressions will have a similarly negative effect in concluding a sales transaction as they will in negotiation. But you have to understand the process and act appropriately.

Firstly, you need to grasp the notion that you are selling; it's what you need to do to survive. Nothing happens in any business without the sale.

Secondly, you need to understand that people buy when they are ready to buy not when you are ready to sell. If there were four words to sum up this book: *it's not about you.* Here it crops up again. You might have the perfect service to solve the problem that you know the Prospective Client has, but unless they realise it and are receptive to what you have to offer to resolve it, you are simply wasting your time.

Think of each Prospective Client out there as if they are on a moving parade of interest, like a conveyor belt. The parade moves quickly and they are exposed to a vast array of marketing messages each day as they move along it – most of which they ignore. Your message has to reach them at the point on the parade when they are receptive to it.

Imagine how this works in your own situation when, say, you are thinking of buying a car. You don't just wake up one morning and decide exactly what make, model and colour of car you're buying in a particular garage for a particular price.

You get a notion that you've got to change the car. And then you start thinking about it, you observe other cars, you gaze at showrooms as you pass, you actually pay attention to ads and you talk to friends, family and acquaintances.

You narrow your field of interest, you start looking at specifics, and you browse the Internet and start getting comparisons and prices. You actually go in to one of the showrooms, walk around and maybe take a test drive.

This is the moving parade of interest. Normally you may not have the slightest interest in cars other than to expect that when you sit in your one it starts and takes you where you want to go. But when you are in the mode of replacing the car you go through a gradual process of heightening interest, during which period the extent to which you might be receptive to messages about cars increases.

And each day of course your interest is dependent on your mood. No matter what point on the parade you're on, if you're hung over, extremely busy or have just had the mother of all rows with your spouse or partner that morning, you may not give a flying fiddle about anything no matter how congruent with your current levels of interest in any particular area.

So, the degree to which a particular message is going to be relevant and meaningful to a Prospective Client depends on them, and how receptive they are to the message at any given moment.

And all of this is precisely why you need to follow up. The chances of your Prospective Client being ready and interested in what you have to say at the moment they first encounter your message is remote; it can happen but again you need to be playing a huge numbers game here.

However, if the person expresses some interest in what it is that you have to say and you then follow up with them appropriately, regularly and consistently, your chances of reaching them at a time when they might be receptive to your message increase dramatically.

As a Real Lawyer you must follow up.

You want to develop a relationship that moves your Prospective Client to being a client; but you can't be so timid and standoffish as to live in the vain hope that after one shot they're going to be so compelled and convinced by what it is that you offer that they're going to be right back to you to find out where to get started.

The people you are going to follow up with are people who have expressed an interest in the first place and have requested you to send them information. And you are going to give them an opportunity to request you to stop at any stage. Not only is this a legal requirement, it's basic common courtesy and sense. But you do have to persist beyond just giving it one feeble go and quitting if you don't get a *yes* straight away.

But you're not into sales or selling you say, you're a professional goddamit. Well whatever you want to call it and however you want to characterise it, you're selling and you need to adapt what works in every other industry into yours to give your business the simple ability to produce that thing which is the life blood of any business: a paying client.

You don't need to be a cheesy salesperson while you're at it. What we are talking about here is a continuation of the provision of helpful and relevant information; consistently and persistently providing something welcome, the most rational and logical response to which is to make contact with you to take the next step.

How do you create a sequence of follow-up?

The simplest and easiest is email. An email follow-up sequence is very easy to set up and can run on autopilot for any number of Prospective Clients.

The sequence can continue to operate indefinitely and each new enquiry entering it will start at the beginning and receive a pre-planned series of emails.

The frequency and duration of the emails that you send will depend very much on what you are trying to achieve, the market you are targeting and the nature of the content.

Take the example of the conveyancing Lead Generation and Lead Conversion process from Chapter 7. In that example the Prospective Client signed up for a helpful guide to the house buying process. The first follow-up communication could be an email sent a few days after they download the guide explaining the timelines in a conveyancing transaction with some handy tips on how to anticipate and avoid delays to ensure that they get the keys to their new home when they want them and how the firm helps them do that. This could be followed by an email the following week explaining how the firm works with them to project manage every aspect of the purchase of their new home to make it flow smoothly. Another email could be sent a week later outlining the costs involved in the transaction, etc. Each email could include links to blog posts or specific pages on your site answering particular queries or providing additional information on specific topics in order to enable further segmentation. For instance whether the Prospective Client is looking to purchase property as an owner occupier or an investor.

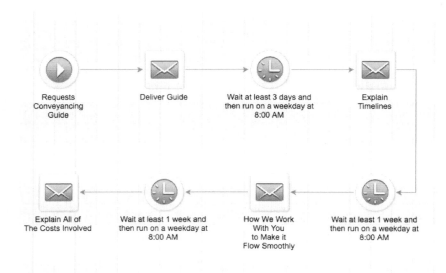

An example of a conveyancing follow up sequence by email.

Whenever using email for marketing purposes always use a reputable autoresponder. There are many out there of varying types and specifications, the costs of which vary from free right on up. Do not try to set up email marketing or an email follow-up sequence using your own office email software or a web-based general email provider. You are far more likely to be categorised as spam as you will not be able to provide the option to unsubscribe. You will be more limited in how you configure and personalise each email without writing each one individually (which kind of defeats the purpose).

The most basic form of autoresponder simply allows you to compile a List of email addresses and names. Having a first name associated with the email address is a very good idea and one I highly recommend. Being able to personalise the email with a first name greeting makes a huge difference to how you go about developing a relationship with the person you are writing to. Sounds corny I know, but it really is important.

However, given the importance of your List to you as a Real Lawyer, I recommend that you use software that will allow you to manage as well as communicate with that List. This involves what is referred to as Contact Relationship Management software (or a CRM). The practice management software that you use in your office may in effect be a form of CRM but I recommend that you use one specifically designed for this purpose and which incorporates an autoresponder to enable you to communicate with the List that is managed via the CRM. Bear in mind too that many of the Prospective Clients you have on the List will not yet be clients and it may not be appropriate or convenient to have them set up in the practice management software, so it is probably a good idea to have these separate unless you have customised software developed specifically to do what you want here.

A CRM with an autoresponder will enable you to manage contacts on your List automatically and track their activity within your follow-up sequences with great accuracy. You can clearly see who has received a particular series of emails or follow-up sequence and the software can start and stop new sequences or move contacts between sequences depending on the actions that they take themselves. You may not need all of this straight away, but it is likely to be the way that you are going to go if you get into this.

Cost can be a very attractive factor when choosing email as a medium; it's free and practically limitless. And done properly email *is* great and incredibly powerful. Just don't go for it because it's cheap; use it for people who want to receive their communication that way.

Consider how many emails you get that you don't read or that you instantly delete. They will generally tend to come from impersonal accounts and do not contain anything that you have any interest in reading.

The emails you are most likely to open and read come from real people who you know and are likely to contain information that you find interesting or valuable. The relationship with the sender and the quality of the content are key factors in the recipient's attitude to the email. It makes the difference between the email being seen as unwanted clutter in an inbox and something that is welcomed and read. You should ensure that emails you send come from an individual at a real email address and you should aim to use the correspondence to develop a relationship of trust with the person receiving the email.

Of course cost is also a factor in the autoresponder software you choose to buy. While there are some free versions that only charge when you get into volume, anything incorporating a proper CRM is going to require investment and most work on an ongoing monthly-charging structure based on the size of your List. Consider the overall capability of any software in terms of what it can do for you. Remember that if you get this working for you properly it can be very powerful and you will want to develop it, so choose software that will give you the scope to do that and remember that you will only ever get what you pay for.

Email is terribly attractive; it's essentially free and easy to reach an awful lot of people instantaneously. Some of the social media pundits are quick to write off email as old hat but it is still one of the most powerful online tools, once you make sure that the emails you send are ones that the person receiving them will want to have in their inbox.

If you're not following up with Prospective Clients systematically right now, email is a good place to start. But as a type of follow-up, email is not enough on its own.

Think of online as the starting point where you first make contact with your Prospective Client; from there you might guide them to an email sequence that will be interesting and beneficial for the prospect. Embedded in your emails you include links to other information and offers. For instance a video with more information on a particular aspect of the topic or an offer to speak with someone who may be able to answer queries on a certain point. When what is offered by one of those links coincides with the prospect's own moving parade of interest: Bingo! That is when you get engagement and action.

If the action is to contact you directly to take the next step or to make an enquiry straight away: great. If not we can break this progression down in further stages.

For example, you provide some basic information in your email sequence; good stuff you understand but owing to the limitations of the medium it has to be relatively brief and perhaps superficial. Then you offer more comprehensive detailed information in hard copy that you are prepared to post to the Prospective Client. This involves a closer step toward engagement and it requires that the person exchange a little more specific information about themselves in return for a bigger benefit; it's a fair deal all the time – or at least it should be. You can't promise good stuff and then not deliver.

Now you have an opportunity to really correspond with the person who has shown interest in what it is that you do. Most, when they make an enquiry with a solicitor, might receive a simple follow-up letter with a quote or, if the firm thinks they are doing great stuff on the marketing side, a glossy brochure. But you now have an opportunity to send something of far greater value. You use the type of information that you have been providing online and you take it to the next level: you can send books, reports, audio or video, the sky really is the limit here.

You don't have to send everything you have together at once, though you can. The first mailing could include a bumper pack for impact; sometimes called a "shock and awe" pack to really impress and get the recipient's attention. But more generally you can spread this out and provide a sequence of contact and information with each step designed ultimately to qualify your Prospective Client more highly and to bring the person closer to making the decision to retain you.

You see now you have a fine body of men and women who go about the country in green vans, on bicycles and with little hand carts, braving wind and rain and vicious dogs to put parcels through letter-boxes to land on people's door mats.

This costs money of course and this is where it gets emotionally and financially a lot more invested than just email. Now you're burning cash as you follow up; but don't lose heart. The stakes got higher but the potential rewards got a lot higher too. An awful lot of email isn't read. But when your Prospective Client walks down the end of their hallway that morning and bends down to pick up that parcel from the floor, you can be pretty sure you have their undivided attention. Everything else on the mat is likely to be bills, flyers and junk. Yours has an opportunity to really stand out now, get opened, read, and acted upon.

It's worth getting into a few practicalities at this point. Think very basic and think very practical. Your message won't get acted upon unless it is read to the point where you request the reader to do something. This is why your content needs to be engaging and interesting. Your content won't be read unless the headline is sufficiently captivating. Your headline won't be read unless they open the envelope. And they won't even get a chance to open the envelope if it doesn't get delivered.

So, you've got to think about how to make sure your envelope or parcel gets delivered. You'd be amazed at how much doesn't. And for instance if you're in a business-to-business (B2B) market, and your envelope has to reach someone inside an organisation, it may not even get past the mailroom.

Then you've got to think about getting your envelope opened. Most people make the fundamental mistake of only thinking about what's *in* the envelope. But the Prospective Client won't even get to that if it looks like junk on the outside. Think about the envelope itself: do you use an actual stamp? Do you use an address label, a printed address or a *handwritten* one? These things make a difference.

It is in this context that you need to think about sequences and what you want to achieve from all of this, both in email, direct mail or whatever type of follow-up you use. You may also choose to follow up on the phone or by a combination of all of these things; which in my view is by far the best, but however you do it, it needs to be systematic and planned.

Your objective has to be central to all of this; what do you want the Prospective Client to do? Then you break this down into steps as to how you might like them to do this. Don't assume they'll follow the same sequence or logical progression that you will. Remember, you and they have completely different levels of knowledge about the problem, that is why they may need you in the first place. Develop your sequence so that the Prospective Client's experience remains congruent throughout. For instance, if the ultimate goal is to have the Prospective Client contact you and you have multiple steps in the sequence designed to lead to that action, once the ultimate goal has been achieved all other intermediate steps should fall away.

Suppose you have a 3-step follow-up sequence of correspondence the primary purpose of which is to have someone contact you for an initial consultation. If after the first step in the sequence, the person makes contact for that initial consultation, you do not want to have your subsequent steps suggesting an initial consultation. However, if no contact is made in the first or second step, you certainly do want your third step to refer to it. An autoresponder integrated with a CRM can manage this for you automatically to ensure that every step in your sequence is congruent with every other step so that when the recipient takes an action, the sequence is adjusted to reflect that if required.

Taken all together, this can look like a lot of work. But you can put each step in place one by one. To develop an email sequence you just need to write one email at a time, you can actually develop a pilot sequence manually and adapt those emails to be added to your autoresponder. For postal follow-up you can start by writing the first letter enclosing the guide or report that the

Prospective Client requested which you then establish as a template letter which you use for every request, and each time you add a step to the sequence you use the material that you have created for that as a further template. You can repurpose content from your blog to create reports or more detailed guides, you can record video or audio based on written content and host it on your website to provide links in emails or burned onto DVDs or CDs to be sent in the post. Gradually you will assemble a comprehensive sequence of email and postal follow-up. You can automate each step in the process through your CRM and autoresponder. As you add each step to the sequence it will be there forever and you won't have to do that work again.

The beauty of a sequence of follow-up is that you now have a process that allows Prospective Clients to qualify themselves to varying degrees to the extent that when they do finally make contact they are largely pre-sold on what you have to offer. The difference with someone just wandering in to kick the tyres and shop on price couldn't be more pronounced.

- ➤ Sales is not negotiation; you must follow up repeatedly.
- ➤ You must make sure that your message reaches your Prospective Client when he or she is receptive to it.
- ➤ Progress from email to hard copy follow-up by post
- ➤ Make sure that your hard copy follow-up is going to be delivered and opened.

➤ Build your follow-up sequences one step at a time and automate them with Contact Relationship Management (CRM) software.

Chapter 13: The Importance of a Regular Newsletter

If you don't like the news, go out and make some of your own.

— Wes "Scoop" Nisker

There is an expression used by direct response marketers of "the herd"; they use the idea of your customer base as a herd and you have to tend the fences around your herd to make sure that they don't stray. To some it is offensive to think of valued clients in this way; some use the expression fans, tribe, etc.

So far I have used the term *customer* interchangeably with *client*. This is quite deliberately intended to challenge your thinking to consider what you do as a business rather than some special thing called a legal practice to which the rules of business do not apply.

But, let's go back to client again for a minute.

The word *client* derives from the notion of a person under the protection of another. A client uses a lawyer to protect his or her interests.

And it is in your interest to protect something equally important: the long-term relationship that you have with that client.

Most lawyers don't do this.

In fact most lawyers moan about the decline in client loyalty. They seem to hark back to a golden age when each person had their 'family solicitor' or some similar long standing retainer to whom they came back religiously whenever they needed to have any legal business done. This was right and proper the traditionalists would say and it is a great shame that it is gone.

But it's a crock and good riddance to it.

First off, if you don't happen to be that incumbent family solicitor to the population at large, how on Earth do you hope to get a start?

Secondly, this took clients for granted. Lawyers had the attitude that clients just had to come back and should be happy to take it the way lawyers wanted to give it; and this was often at excessive cost with no customer service worth speaking of.

And thirdly, and in the context of this chapter most importantly, lawyers did not do anything to foster and develop that client loyalty that they say they valued so much; so why the hell should they be in the slightest bit surprised that they lost it.

How do you nurture this loyalty? By the basic act of keeping in contact and the simplest and most effective way for a Real Law firm to do so is a regular client newsletter.

You may yawn and turn to the next chapter when I tell you this. Surely there must be sexier, snazzier, and more hi-tech things that you could be doing before you get to plain old printed newsletters sent in the post. But you'd be missing out on something big if you did. This works; big style.

Did you notice a word in the last paragraph? "Yawn"?

If your newsletter makes them yawn, you are wasting your time writing it, printing it and spending a shed load of money to have it delivered (because remember it's got to be printed and sent by post – this the ultimate form of regular client retention follow-up).

Think for a minute about a regular newsletter that you receive in the post each month: your Gazette. First you look to see if *you're* in it. Then you look at the pictures to see if anyone you know is in it. Then you look at the regulatory section to see if you know anyone who's been sanctioned or struck off. Then you read the news bits. Then you scan the articles and if there's one in an area that is relevant to you, you may read it there and then, or mark it and read it later (which you rarely do.)

You probably open the Gazette when opening the post, so there's usually of ton of other immediate work that needs to be done and therefore you may not have the luxury of being able to read it there and then when you get it, other than to scan the interesting bits. When you don't look at it there and then, you probably don't return to it that often, unless there's something really interesting and compelling that you remember to come back to.

Your newsletter is the same in the hands of whoever receives it. You have an opportunity to speak to them in their hallway or kitchen where you have their complete attention. The other post arriving generally consists of bills, junk mail and unwelcome or boring correspondence. To get something that they look forward to in the post is a real treat. Something interesting or entertaining is sure to grab their attention at the end of a busy day when they rifle through the junk in the post box or on the door mat before throwing most of it in the bin.

But if it isn't interesting it is going to be seen as junk mail like all the rest and cast into the recycling without even a cursory glance. This is your challenge and your opportunity.

First off, no-one wants to read an article about why they should make their will, an enduring power of attorney, a shareholder's agreement or whatever. *You* may care about this; this might be business you wish to attract and there may be good reasons why people should be reminded about this. Just don't make it the central focus of your newsletter. Similarly, weighty legal subjects and important cases are no good; *you* might find them interesting, but your clients won't.

Instead, think about what is interesting in your clients' lives; what are they likely to read about? Think the features section of a popular magazine or weekend newspaper. This is going into people's homes and on to their coffee tables, make it something they might actually read, find interesting and pass on to a family member or a friend.

Apart from that the most important thing to put into your newsletter (and all of your marketing efforts the truth be told) is *your personality.* The first time I travelled to Arlington in the US to attend Ben Glass's *Great Legal Marketing Summit* I was amazed when Glass came on stage for his opening address and told us that he was going to show us his best ever pulling marketing piece. He is one of the top direct response marketers and *the* best lawyer doing this stuff. When he said he was going to reveal his best piece as tested by him over years, spending fortunes marketing in one of the most competitive environments on the planet, I thought this is going to be good. This is going to be worth travelling across the Atlantic and all of the associated time and expense.

And what did he reveal? A cinema-screen-sized photograph of him and his extended family.

His personal story, his family and everything going on with it and his life is what he has used as the centre of his marketing. He is just himself and he is quite comfortable putting that out there. And his clients, and people who have never been his clients but have the potential to be, love him as a result. They love keeping up with developments, being on the inside track; seeing that Glass and his family and his team and their families are real people with real lives just like everyone else.

The more they see the real person behind the "lawyer" and can empathise with that person and the life they lead, they come to like them and as humans we are comfortable doing business with people we know, like and trust. When people see you as you really are in your newsletter, they're no longer thinking about you as a lawyer but as a person.

Moreover, the strongest unique selling proposition that you can adopt is that you are *you*. The relationship of trust that you have with your clients is something that they cannot get from anyone else and who you are is central to it.

Now this doesn't mean that you have to run an exposé of your private life and that of your family and your staff in your newsletter. But you can make it personal and interesting and with a little thought you can make it your own. When you think about this a little, it actually makes the job of assembling the content a whole lot easier. It's much easier to pull together some photos from a fun event with a few snappy captions than it is to sit down and write some turgid article about the benefits to be had from registering rights of way.

So, make sure that the majority of the content is non-legal in nature and make it personal. I know, I know, I am now contradicting everything I have said previously about it *not being about you* and it being relevant to your target market.

Let me explain.

You're not trying to sell or show off what you know here. That's boring. And it not being about you in this context means it's not about what you want to get from the newsletter (new business; that you might be tempted to promote) but rather it's about what your clients and Prospective Clients will find *interesting*, and people find news, and stories about people's lives, interesting.

How do you go about creating content? Well, start with a folder where you can gather ideas. Keep it around your desk or have a folder on your computer. Keep an eye out for things that you think might have potential for the newsletter. When you see something happening that you think might make a good story, take a photo on your phone. There are countless apps for smartphones that can help with this. I use Evernote on my iPhone and whenever I see something that I think could be useful as content or might give me an idea for content, I snap a picture of it and drop it into a notebook in Evernote I've created for newsletter material.

In terms of ideas start with your own stuff; things going on in the office, in your life, in the lives of the people that work with you; things going on in the community; that type of thing. Then think like the features editor of a weekend newspaper magazine supplement. I'll bet you someone in your office is a keen cook and would love to share recipes, there's probably a gardener on the team who can produce tips; you can include regular slots on fitness, pets, charity events or causes that are important to you; the key here is to make it authentic. This will actually make it far easier to produce because it is coming from you naturally.

The other source of content for your newsletter is your clients. Remember when I mentioned the Gazette, the one time it'll really get my attention is if I'm in it; even my kids will look at it then. Same goes for the local paper. If you put your clients in your newsletter, they'll love you and it and will be sure to show it to their friends. For instance, if you've got a client with a business, or any local business, run a feature on their business in the newsletter. They'll really appreciate the exposure to your List. Then give them a framed copy for their premises and a stack of them to give away at their front desk; they'll be delighted to if it's showing off their business in a good light.

Being in a magazine makes celebrities of people. I know, the world is a shallow, shallow place, but we might as well learn to live with it. Even though it's just your firm's newsletter, if you do it right it can make you and your people and the other people who feature in it into mini-celebrities. It can even be used to enhance your people's expert status in the process; all you have to do is make sure that you don't break the golden rule and bore people in the process.

Now when it comes to compiling the content for your newsletter, you've got a folder full of ideas and a load of pictures on your phone. Writing a small piece on each is not going to be taxing. Keep it light and write like you speak using an easy conversational style. Put captions on some interesting photographs. Before you know it you are going to be stuck for space and editing is going to be your problem.

OK, so that's a bird's eye overview on content. The next question is medium.

You've got to have a print newsletter. You can email around a pdf or you can use various types of autoresponder options to send eZine type email newsletters, but I would only do so in addition to, rather than instead of, a print newsletter. People get too much email already, generic newsletter emails are unlikely to be read or even opened.

No, this has to be printed ink on paper and sent in the post. If you think about it, this is the best possible type of follow-up mentioned in the previous chapter. It's regular and continuous and it's interesting. It keeps you in the minds of people who have been willing to pay for your services in the past and makes them aware of how you can help them and their friends and family. That is the ultimate objective of your newsletter, to ensure that your existing clients will keep coming back to you and refer others.

The final point is frequency. At the time of writing, I send ours quarterly but you could also go monthly. In terms of content creation and cost I find quarterly a good balance. The important thing is to produce it consistently and regularly. You'll know it's working is when you get asked when the next issue is due.

> ➢ Foster and develop client loyalty with your newsletter; do not take it for granted or think that it will happen by itself.

The Importance of a Regular Newsletter

> ➤ Make your newsletter interesting. Make it something to look forward to.
>
> ➤ Put your personality into your newsletter; let everyone see the people behind the lawyers.
>
> ➤ Make the majority of the content non-relevant to your practice areas. It's not about what you want, it's about what your readers will find interesting.
>
> ➤ Use your newsletter to make celebrities of your staff, your clients and other businesses.
>
> ➤ Use print and ink, and send it regularly.

Part III

The Tools to Build With

In Part I of this book we have looked at the fundamentals, getting your head and the basics of your business right. Your rock or solid ground.

In Part II we looked at the foundation, the platform that you establish on that rock on top of which you will build the superstructure of your business.

Now you need the tools; the specific techniques that you will use to generate traffic, the life blood of any business: Prospective Clients.

That's what we look at in Part III.

Chapter 14: Organic Traffic: SEO

Content is king, but marketing is queen, and runs the household.

– Gary Vaynerchuk

SEO stands for search engine optimisation.

People searching the web are doing just that, searching. They could be anywhere on the moving parade of interest and may not necessarily be close to a buying decision. Therefore, bear in mind that "free" traffic from organic SEO may bring visitors to your site but the quality of those visitors may not necessarily be any good. Never make the mistake of being taken in solely by traffic numbers, in terms of hits to your website. Think of HITS as an acronym: "How Idiots Track Success". Quality is far more important than quantity.

In order to navigate the web we have things called search engines. They enable us to find what we are looking for by typing in (or increasingly just speaking) queries. The search engines have highly secretive algorithms that they use to trawl the web based on your search terms to produce a list of results the search engine deems most relevant to your query ranked in order of relevance from 1 to however many. As I write this the search term "solicitors Ireland" returned 2,160,000 results in 0.38 seconds.

In the face of so many search results most people will never look very much further than the first few on the very first page; the search engine results page or SERP. The ranking of results on these pages is very important in determining whether anyone ever sees stuff that is relevant to their search terms.

Search engine optimisation (SEO) then is that practice or set of practices that web developers engage in to ensure that their websites are optimised for search engines; i.e. to give them the best chance of ranking highly for the search terms that the website owners wish to rank for. As you can probably imagine, it's big business and has been for years. The traffic that you get from SEO can be thought of as the "natural" traffic that comes from people searching the web and is therefore referred to as "organic" traffic; i.e. you don't pay for it directly.

SEO has undergone many changes over the years and continues to do so. Google is in business to make money; its primary source of revenue is selling advertising to people on Google to look for other things (we'll come to this advertising later).

But people only use Google because it's brilliant at what it does and because of this has become so prevalent that it is the only search engine for many.

So in order for Google to maintain its position as the search engine that everyone uses (and thereby to ensure that it has a large and growing audience for the ad space it sells in the process) Google must ensure that the search results that it provides are the most relevant for the person carrying out the search. In short, Google's primary aim is to ensure the best possible user experience: that they find what they are looking for as quickly as possible. That is all that matters to them. You need to really grok[2] this.

---

[2] Yes, it is a word. (See the Glossary.)

Therefore as a Real Lawyer you should align your interests with Google's in so far as you can. Google is determined to provide the best possible user experience; you should do the same.

Make your website answer the questions that your Prospective Clients are likely to be asking. Create lots of valuable content written by and intended to be read by human beings. Do this in writing, on audio and on video. Create content that is worthy of your expert status. Do not take this as permission to write and speak like a lawyer; don't ever do that. Convey the expert knowledge you have in a way that will help the visitor and answer their query. Do not duplicate content or stuff your site full of any old content because more is better; be selective and edit wisely. Always think in terms of the user experience as the search engines will continually be striving to serve up the best and most relevant content to their users as swiftly and easily as possible.

So, the quality of your content is vital, the next thing is the topic. This has to be relevant to what your Prospective Client is looking for. Which is linked to the keywords you use in your content.

Reliable keyword research in Ireland is difficult, because the search volumes are so low. On top of this Google have increasingly restricted your ability to see what keywords people are using to visit your site. Google AdWords (which we will come to in Chapter 16) provides tools that can help with general keyword research but the tools are now very focussed for use on the AdWords platform and do not provide the type of detailed information on search traffic for individual terms that they used to.

So you will need to start with some educated guess work on the keywords that are important for the areas you wish to rank for and work from there. One very quick and easy way to research the words that people are searching for is to use Google's autocomplete function in the search box. When you type anything into the search box in Google, Google will start to give you suggestions on what you may be searching for based on the words you've started to type. While you will not get specific data on search volumes for individual terms through this method, it will show you quickly and easily whether anyone else is using those terms in their search queries on Google.

In practising SEO, solicitors are trying to get their websites ranked for the terms that are important to the *solicitors*. But in this process Google doesn't care about the solicitors; it only cares about the searchers – your Prospective Clients – and providing them with the results that are most relevant to them.

Does this sound familiar? *It's not about you.*

The terms and keywords that *you* would like your website to rank for are not important; what's important are the terms and keywords that your Prospective Clients are using in their searches and then making sure that your content will answer the queries of your Prospective Client in the terms they are using themselves.

When thinking about terms and keywords that might be relevant to your Prospective Clients bear in mind that the more specific you are for your Prospective Client the better; choose the same terms they are using in their searches.

High level generic terms or vanity keywords like "solicitor" or "divorce" will always have higher traffic volumes. As you get more specific the volumes will decrease but the potential quality of those searching for the more specific terms will increase. "Child custody solicitor Killarney" or "solicitor for will disputes in

Galway" will have lower volumes but anyone searching on those terms is going to have a very specific need. If your content addresses that, any visitor to your site searching on those terms is likely to be very interested in the information you have to provide.

The ultimate extension of this keyword refinement process is in what are known as long-tail keywords. If you were to show keywords on a graph by popularity of searches from highest to lowest, the front of the graph would peak with the most popular keywords with the highest volume and would then trail off in a long tail. While you might have thousands searching for high level generic keywords, you may have only one or two searching for keywords appearing in the long tail of the graph. However, the quality of those searching for the long-tail keywords is very high in that they have a very specific need which they have defined in detail. You just have to create content that speaks directly to them in those terms. Here are a couple of examples:

In each of the examples above just typed at random into an empty Google search box you will see that Google has suggested completed phrases based on the keywords entered. This gives a very good indication that people are searching on these terms; the volumes may be low but the quality of those searching in terms of their interest in the subject matter very high.

So you have to create valuable content that is relevant to your Prospective Clients and one way in which Google determines your relevance is based on the keywords contained within it.

Another way in which Google determines value is by seeing how others naturally link to your content. When real people link to content and share it via social media, etc. this is one good indicator of its value. The important word in this paragraph is *naturally*. Links to your site should come about naturally because people are motivated to link to it because of the value of the content to them. Don't try to create links artificially.

Back in the early days of SEO it was possible to game the system. You could stuff your web page with keywords that would make it look more relevant to Google than might otherwise be the case. Content was written for search engines rather than real people. And it was relatively easy to generate links from all over the Internet to your website even though the links themselves may have been complete rubbish. Google's wise to all this now and a whole lot more, and it is continually refining and updating its algorithm to weed out the sites it sees as abusing the system. Don't chance it.

So, let's assume that we do it all correctly. There is this idea that SEO is free and that by using legitimate SEO techniques in a way that is approved by Google we can generate oodles of website traffic that will lead to more new business then we can shake a big stick at. Not quite.

First off, nothing is free. You are always paying: either with your cash; your time; your opportunity cost; or the quality of your performance. There is no getting around this. There are some that go around smugly saying that they get tons of free organic traffic from SEO and if you are willing to believe them then more luck to them; but it's not free. It came at a price. It's just a question of how you wish to pay it.

In all of this think ROI. This is the most important concept to get clear in your mind in everything that you do with your marketing. Cost is irrelevant if the ROI is right (and of course you know all your numbers and can sustain cash flow). When your cost is free the ROI is infinite; but it's never free so just get comfortable with how you'd like to pay.

The other thing about SEO is that it's liable to change and we have no idea when or how it is going to change. Google releases updates named after creatures like pandas, penguins and hummingbirds constantly and you never know about them until afterwards. These updates can involve changes to penalise what are known as "black hat" or "spammy" practices (*black hat* being bad while *white hat* is good and *spam* being the term used to describe everything dodgy on the web from email to links). What you might innocently think is perfectly compliant may get deemed by Google's algorithm to be an infringement.

The bottom line in much of your marketing and in SEO in particular is that valuable content is king. Keep producing high quality content that is relevant to your Prospective Clients and keep your nose clean with Google. After that treat organic SEO as a bonus and never become overly reliant on any one source of traffic.

The quality of your content is down to you: your knowledge of your specialism and the Prospective Clients that you wish to attract and your ability to answer the questions that are important to them in their own terms. As for what Google wants, keep it simple, just ask them. To find out what Google wants, search in Google for webmaster SEO tools and a link to Google's support section is likely to appear top of the list. Go there and do what they say.

> - You cannot control SEO and no-one outside of Google knows how it works. Be wary of it, do not depend on it and do not try to game the system.
> - Google's primary aim is to provide the best possible user experience.
> - Align yourself with this aim and produce valuable content that is relevant for your Prospective Clients. Always think in terms of the user, not what you are looking to get out of it.
> - Create content for humans not search engines. Create content worthy of your expert status. Avoid duplicate content and content stuffed with what you think are important keywords.
> - The more specific the keywords you use the lower the volumes searching but the higher the quality.

Chapter 15: Social Media

Be yourself. Everyone else is already taken.

— Oscar Wilde

Social media covers everything from blogging on your own blog through to sharing content on social media platforms like Facebook, Twitter, Google+, YouTube and LinkedIn.

You can of course simply interact on these social media platforms and create content there directly, you can post directly on Facebook and Twitter. You can also curate and share content from other sources, links and references to other interesting, useful or entertaining content from elsewhere on the web.

Social media can produce very dramatic results, in a very short time, at very little cost, if you know what you're doing. So much so that there has been a veritable social media marketing Klondike.

In any gold rush there are a few prospectors that strike it rich and a vast number who get the gold fever when they see what the successful or lucky ones have done but end up spending a lot of effort and money with nothing to show for it. The ones that always make money are the service providers: the shovel and pick sellers, horse dealers and saloon proprietors.

The social media gold rush is no different. The people providing the infrastructure and service providers like social media marketing consultants are the ones most consistently making money from it. So, while social media might have a lot of potential, as a Real Lawyer you need to proceed with a little care in an area with a lot of distracting hype much of which is generated by people with big vested interests.

The type of marketing discussed throughout this book revolves around creating valuable content for your Prospective Clients. This is known as content marketing, and for this the blogging base is the best. Don't make it the main or only thing you do, but you do need to create content anyway and once you do so it is very easy to re-purpose that content and use it in multiple ways. Having a presence on each social media platform then gives you multiple channels through which you can get your content out there. Done right, it can get you a lot of exposure very quickly.

The key, however, is that you are very clear on what you are trying to achieve with all of this: what is the action you want the user to end up taking if he or she does engage and read your post, listen to your audio or watch your video. You must be clear about your objective and the action that you wish your Prospective Client to take at the end of it all.

The most important aspect of this process is the direction of the flow of traffic. Remember your objective here: to get traffic to flow to your website/blog, onto your List so that you can follow up with them. This is a one-way flow of traffic. Whatever anyone may tell you about engagement and sharing and all that other good stuff, this has to be the direction of the flow. You want to get anyone interacting with your content to your main website where you provide them with a compelling reason to sign up to your List.

The Flow of Traffic from Social Media
Must *Always* be *To* Your List

You create valuable content on your blog and you point to it via social media to drive traffic to your blog to read that content. There you need a call to action. At the end of each blog post you have a call to action urging the reader to take the next step: to leave you their contact details in return for something more. This will be your offer of value; something relevant to the post and providing more detailed or valuable content: a report, book, video, audio, webinar, email course, whatever. And then you follow up with them.

The purpose of your use of social media is to get traffic *to* your site, not to take traffic *away* from your site. Therefore, when you do get the Prospective Client to your blog or your landing page with your call to action do not have a link to Twitter, Facebook or LinkedIn taking them straight off your site. Social media should have no presence on the landing pages on your site to which you send traffic from social media or other traffic sources: these should only have a compelling call to action based on an offer to contact you directly or to sign up to your List.

Ultimately the objective of everything you do on social media will be exactly the same as what you do elsewhere: you'll just be using a different medium to do it.

Once you are clear on this overarching objective, the next thing is authenticity. If you decide to use social media, doing so in such a way that understands the *social* aspect of the medium is vital. In this respect you have to find your voice for each platform and then you have to be authentic in the way you use it. The social media presences that work best tend to be clearly represented by real people who engage in a natural way, similar to how they would if you met them in person. You wouldn't last long at a *social* event just talking about yourself and handing out business cards, and the same rules apply on social media. You also need to be aware of the "house style" of each platform. Facebook is very casual and relaxed, Twitter is fast paced and highly reactive to news and popular culture, LinkedIn is completely business focussed and Google+ tends to be where the early adopters and innovators, the online cool-kids, hang out. Your voice on each should suit the situation and also come across as natural and authentically you.

You need to use each medium in a way that suits the type of conversations taking place there and allow yourself to come across as *yourself*.

The next thing is the ROI. On the face of it social media is free. But the way in which you are going to be paying for this one is in time: time spent creating the content and time spent in actually using the media. You must plan this time carefully and measure the return that you are getting from this investment. The decisions you take on the role which social media should play in your overall marketing effort must, as with every other medium, be based on the ROI you get from it.

So, let's take an example: say you have a practice area that you want to promote. You think of 10 blog posts that you can write on the subject over the course of a month. Say it's family law and you chose 10 titles such as:

- How do I avoid the financial costs of separation?
- How can I afford a good lawyer for my separation?
- What are the first things I need to do when I decide to separate?
- My spouse has always taken control of the finances; how will I cope if I separate?
- Is there any advantage in being the person who starts the separation process?
- What should I do if I'm having problems with my marriage?
- When should I think about talking to a lawyer if I'm having problems with my marriage?
- Can mediation work if my spouse always dominates everything we do?
- How do I protect my kids from being hurt if I separate?
- How do I prepare for separation?

Then you write them, say 500-750 words each. (That's a handy bit of writing, so already you can see how you're paying for this one. But again, if you do it cleverly, this content can be reused in many ways.)

Next you post these on your blog every few days throughout the month. It doesn't have to be regular as clockwork but your blog should look like it's getting fresh and new content all of the time. Once your blog forms part of your main site, the regular addition of fresh content will contribute to your SEO efforts and if people see that blog content via social media, then share and link back to it, in turn this will all contribute to the natural SEO that was covered in the last chapter.

Now, you take each blog post and you put it out via each social media platform that you feel is appropriate for it.

You can highlight aspects of the blog post that you feel would appeal to the Facebook audience and post a link to it there. Make it interesting; give your audience a good reason for taking a look. Why is the post interesting? Why should anyone take a look at this? What secrets have you revealed or important information have you uncovered that will help or interest the reader. You'll need a good headline to catch the reader's attention.

You then do something similar on Twitter, LinkedIn and Google+ except with each platform you tailor the tone and frequency of the post to suit the medium and the audience. On Twitter things move very quickly and a post that on Facebook might be seen by many may disappear in the Twitter feed before anyone has a chance to see it. So you may need to be creative about how you post the link on Twitter in different ways at different times. On LinkedIn the frequency is less hectic and the tone is completely business focussed. B2C posts that will go down well on Facebook and Twitter may look odd on LinkedIn, and vice versa.

You can automate how you post across social media platforms with applications like Hootsuite which will send multiple posts at pre-scheduled times. This needs to be done carefully to avoid seeming scattergun in nature which will undermine your credibility and authenticity. For instance, the frequency with which you might post on Twitter would come across all wrong if you were to post simultaneously on Facebook on each occasion.

And remember the direction of the flow and the objective in all of this: you send out posts through each of the channels which you have created via your presence on each of the social media platforms. These posts contain a link back to your blog or your website. That blog post or landing page on your website contains a clear call to action based on a compelling offer designed to make the Prospective Client either contact you directly or exchange their contact details for valuable information. The whole purpose of your social media activity is to generate traffic for Lead Generation.

Now, social media is not just about broadcasting your content; it's about two-way communication. To use the medium effectively you need to engage with your community and not just pump out messages about you. And as you develop relationships on each platform you may get creative in how you involve others to encourage participation. If you regularly Like and share other's posts they may be happy to share yours in return once you let them know they're out there or involve them in a conversation. Social media is big on reciprocity.

Of course if you're creating your content the right way in the first place it won't be about you, will it? It will be designed to be helpful and interesting for your Prospective Clients.

The question of time spent engaging with your community is a little more difficult; you need to establish very clearly how good a use of your time this turns out to be based on the ROI you gain from the activity. In order to do this you need to plan and measure two things very carefully: the time you spend on social media and the results you get from it. Be clear on whether you are going on there for news, entertainment or fun, in which case do it in your free time to your heart's content. During business hours be very ruthless and disciplined in how you use your time on social media and make that time accountable for results. Determine the productivity of that time based on those results.

Apart from Facebook, Twitter, Google+ and LinkedIn, the other social media platform that deserves individual mention is YouTube. YouTube is more than a social media site, it is the second biggest search engine in the world after Google (and of course YouTube is owned by Google). Huge numbers of people search for answers to everything on YouTube.

Video is an incredibly powerful medium and it isn't restricted to YouTube. Video may be hosted in a wide variety of ways on your website but YouTube is an exceptionally cheap, easy and effective way of promoting it. Video content enables you to demonstrate your expertise and your ability to explain what you know in a very approachable manner in plain English. A Prospective Client can get a feel for who you are and what you are really like through video that just isn't possible in any other way. They can get to know you before either of you have to commit to taking time out to meet in a consultation or even speak on the phone.

Good quality video is now easy and cheap to produce. Video should definitely form part of the mix of valuable content that you create and is in fact just another way to re-purpose content that you have already created in other media. For instance you can video answers to FAQs that you've covered elsewhere or do a quick video run through of something you've covered in a blog post. Some people like to watch, some people like to listen, some people like to read. You should provide them with the option to engage with your content in the way that suits them best. Using video via YouTube adds an important additional dimension to your content and gives you a presence in a powerful search engine to boot.

Where social media can work particularly well is in leveraging news stories that are relevant to your practice areas and in getting great PR and media coverage as a result. Social media also provides what seems to me to be a unique opportunity to meet and build real relationships with journalists and others in the media which can in turn be used to good effect when you do have something to say or an opinion in which the media might be interested.

"News jacking" is a technique that you can use to piggy back on popular stories in the news via social media. You can use the interest that exists in a particular story to get exceptionally high levels of interest in a blog post or video that you promote through social media. If you do this cleverly, the sky is literally the limit. Once you see a story in the news about a subject that comes within your area of expertise you start blogging on this subject with good and intelligent expert comment related and referring directly to the story. Timing is important here and you need to get your content out fast as the news cycle moves quickly. Journalists will be researching the story online. Once your content provides them with useful context and analysis that they can use and refer to they may contact you for comment. This can produce valuable PR and develop your position as an expert in your area. This creates a positive feedback loop that you can harness to great effect. Your appearance in the press, on radio or TV becomes a story for your blog to be put out via social media and on and on it goes. And of course journalists won't be the only ones researching this story; once the story is in the news Prospective Clients will be driven online too, searching for the very topic about which you are creating and sharing valuable content.

One very practical example of this came from the PIP breast implant recall. My partner John specialises in defective product liability and noticed this story breaking very early on. He had been blogging previously on the lack of regulation in the cosmetic surgery industry and had had articles featured in the Farmer's Journal and the Irish Times. When the PIP story broke, John started blogging on it immediately and we promoted these blog posts heavily on social media, primarily Twitter.

Journalists noticed the content and John started getting calls. He was initially featured in the Sunday Independent as the story broke, the same journalist returned to John repeatedly as the story unfolded for comment and he featured in the paper on a number of occasions over that time. We used the articles in the Sunday Independent as the basis for further posts on the blog and social media.

Social Media

John was subsequently contacted for media interviews and appeared on national radio on Savage Sunday on Today FM and Joe Duffy's LiveLine on RTE Radio 1. He was also interviewed on local radio on Cork's 96FM and West Cork's C103.

As each interview happened we used this to create further content for the blog which we posted on social media. This created a serious snowball effect which culminated with John appearing on national TV on RTE's PrimeTime to be interviewed as an expert in the area when they ran an expose on the PIP breast implant scandal. In an intensive period of a few months the campaign produced extraordinary publicity for an otherwise obscure small rural firm and lead to a very large number of new instructions from all over the country.

This may seem an isolated and unique incident. However, a couple of years previously we had similar success in gaining nationwide media coverage on the DePuy Hip Implant Recall which lead directly to multiple new instructions.

News jacking works but it's time critical and issue specific. You've got to be vigilant and ready to act quickly to produce content that is highly relevant to the story of the day and also relates to work you want to attract.

Finally, a further word about ROI. You really have to apply it ruthlessly here too. Not all of your attempts at getting PR via social media posts on news stories are going to hit pay dirt and there will be a certain amount of wastage. The time you spend developing relationships with journalists online beforehand will be a telling factor here. If you are present on social media and able and willing to answer questions that are asked about your area of expertise you are much more likely to be seen as someone to go to when a question arises. Then your post on a topic in an area in which you are a recognised expert will be much more likely to stand out.

As with all other time spent on social media you have to manage and record the time you spend developing those relationships and measure it against the results you get from it. In this instance when reputation-enhancing PR exposure is the objective you might consider appearances in the press, on radio or on TV as positive results for ROI purposes.

> Social media is free and popular but you need to plan and record the time you spend on it carefully; this is your investment.

> Be clear on your objectives and measure the results you obtain from it; know the return you are getting on your investment in social media.

> The direction of the flow should be one way only: towards List building. From the web, to social media, to your blog, to a sign up to your email List or hard copy mailing List.

> Include a clear call to action at the end of each blog post to sign up to an email List so that you can continue to follow up subsequently.

> Social media should only ever be used to get traffic *to* your site, not to take traffic away from it.

> YouTube is the biggest search engine after Google; use it to harness the power of video.

Social Media

➤ Use social media to get PR on stories or expertise that you can share that are relevant to stories in the news.

Chapter 16: Paid Online Methods

A man who stops advertising to save money is like a man who stops a clock to save time.

— Henry Ford

Pay-per-click (PPC)

So far we've been looking at generating traffic from SEO and social media, both ostensibly free. However, that free ride *ain't free*; it's a question of how you pay.

Pay-per-click is a different animal. It is, as it says on the tin, advertising on the Internet which you pay for each time (but only when) a Prospective Client clicks on it. Ingenious, no?

And while our efforts in SEO and social media are ultimately concerned with traffic generation too, there are a number of fundamental differences between the type of traffic that comes from each of those sources and that which comes from pay-per-click advertising. SEO is based on search: the traffic that comes from this source will tend to be researching on the web. Social media traffic flows from the interaction or engagement of others with the content you put out. Traffic you receive from that source may not be in any immediate need of your services and may just find your content interesting.

PPC advertising is different. It is interruption based: your ad is seeking to interrupt someone from something else that they are doing or looking for. This means that you may get a lower response rate to an ad than to non-commercial content that is interesting or engaging in its own right. However, there is a very important difference: a person clicking on an ad is more likely to be a buyer and a buyer with an immediate need of that service. Otherwise they'd probably have just ignored the ad.

The other main difference between PPC advertising and SEO or social media is that while on the latter two you have been paying with your time, on the former you will paying in hard cash once people do click on your ads. And you can burn a lot of cash very quickly with PPC advertising. This is no reason not to do it but it is a reason to be extremely vigilant and to design campaigns that will produce measurable results from the start which you then monitor closely to ensure that only those producing positive ROI are allowed to continue. Done in this way, PPC is a very valuable part of your traffic generation toolkit. Moreover, unlike SEO and social media, you don't have to create masses of content or spend time developing large networks of relationships in the first place to get it to work effectively for you. Once you have a budget to spend you can deploy it at will. Finally, as a PPC advertiser you are in a very different relationship with the search engines and social media sites to someone simply seeking free traffic, you are a paying customer and it is in their interests that you get value for money over the longer term once you do it properly.

PPC advertising can be broken down into four main types:

1. Google AdWords (and Microsoft's Bing equivalent)

2. Social Media Advertising (very different to social media marketing)

3. Banner ads, and

4. Remarketing.

Let's take a look at each one in turn:

Google AdWords

AdWords is by far the largest and most mature of the pay-per-click platforms. And much of what we say here about how AdWords works will apply with slight variations to the other forms of PPC.

So what are we talking about? When a Prospective Client searches online, the results of their search are shown as a search engine results page (a SERP).

This SERP contains a list of results in order of priority from 1 downwards. These are referred to as the organic search results.

Immediately above the organic search results for the Top 3 entries there are *paid* results which show either in a slightly different colour to the organic results or have a little label to show that they are ads. To most people it is quite clear that these are paid results or ads. On a desktop computer you will also see paid results or ads over on the right hand side of the screen whereas the organic results will appear on the left hand side below the Top 3 paid ads.

But you say, "Yes, of course, I know that; any idiot can see that these are ads and that's why I ignore them whenever I'm looking for something." Fair point; people who are just searching for information do ignore and filter out the ads. It depends on where they are on their own parade of interest at that particular moment. But if your ad is relevant to what they're interested in it may in fact present the solution to their problem in a way that they may not have even been able to articulate or conceive of themselves. Then the chance of them clicking on the ad is very high. *And*, here's the interesting bit: someone responding to an ad is a very different person to someone who is just doing research. Someone who responds to an ad is a *buyer*, or at least a Prospective Client.

That's how the ads appear on the screen, but these ads don't just appear at random. Google doesn't just throw them up there in the hope that people will see something that's relevant to them and they just might click on it. When people are using Google's search engine to browse the Internet, Google uses the search terms that they have entered to tailor the ads that they are shown as well as the search engine results that appear, this is called the *search network*. When people are just looking at web pages and using online services like G-mail, Google uses any information that it may have about their search history and preferences (and it has an awful lot) to show ads that it thinks are most relevant to that person; this is called the *display network.*

And so in using AdWords you do something very similar to SEO in that you identify keywords and phrases that Prospective Clients are likely to be searching for in their quest for a solution to their problem, and you associate these with your AdWords campaigns. The key difference to SEO is that in this instance Google wants you to find the keywords that might position your ads more effectively so that you'll keep spending and it gives you powerful tools for doing so.

To get started with AdWords you just need to create an AdWords account. To actually start running ads, you'll need to provide credit card details, however you can access the tools without doing that. As with everything in the Google universe, your AdWords account will be based within your Google account which you will access using a G-mail address. If you haven't already got a separate one for your business set up a new one; don't use a personal G-mail account if you have one already. You may wish to give others access to this account in due course and you may need to link the account to other services, so create one that is exclusively used for your business.

Once you've got a Google account just type *adwords* into the search box on Google or go to www.adwords.google.com where you'll be prompted to either create a new account or log in to an existing account.

If you don't have an existing account, you will be taken through a welcome set-up by AdWords where you will provide details of your website and a daily budget as you go through the set-up process. Don't worry, you won't actually start spending anything until you submit credit card details and set a campaign in motion, so you can experiment with the account and use the tools without going live.

From your account you will see the Tools tab, and then select Keyword Planner. Here you will be given options to search for new keyword ideas, get historical statistics such as search volumes for keywords and view traffic forecasts to get an idea how a given keyword might perform for a given bid and budget.

The AdWords structure is based upon a hierarchy which starts with the campaign level at the top. You may have any number of different campaigns. Campaigns are then broken down in ad groups and ad groups in turn are made up of individual ads. For instance, you might have a campaign on a particular practice area, ad groups focussed on particular services within that practice area and ads focussed on different problems these services can help solve and the keywords people are likely to be using to search for them in the individual ad groups.

As with so many things, the level of detail into which you are willing to go here will be key to your results. The more generic and broadly based your campaigns are at each level the less likely your ad is going to be particularly relevant to anyone. Going granular and getting very specific will be much more effective, but that requires a lot more work and effort. However, always bear in mind that this is work that most of your competitors will be unwilling to do and effort that they will be unwilling to expend; the more you embrace the complexity, the deeper the competitive advantage you will have.

Say for example a general practice were to set up an AdWords campaign where they designed ads around the firm's name and location directing traffic to the firm's home page and using keywords around the areas the firm practices in: conveyancing keywords, probate keywords, family law keywords, litigation keywords etc. This campaign may generate traffic, but it is going to be impossible to match the visitor who has clicked the ad with the service that they are interested in and the page that they are being sent to, which may well just be the firm's home page, will reflect this and be very generic. And of course advertising based solely around a firm's name is wasteful brand advertising in the first place.

The same firm could develop a much more effective campaign by breaking the campaign down into targeted segments. They could have a conveyancing campaign with ads designed for house buyers and sellers sending the visitor to a landing page specifically dealing with conveyancing issues. The keywords used in that sub-campaign would relate solely to conveyancing issues, and the ads in the ad groups associated with that campaign would reflect the issues associated with the keywords that the people interested in those issues are searching for rather than the firm's name or features. They could have similar sub-campaigns for probate, family law and litigation matters.

Indeed, this can be segmented further in that the conveyancing campaign could be segmented into house buyers and house sellers. Again the keywords in each of these sub-campaigns can be far more targeted and specific as can the ads shown based on these keywords and the landing page that the visitor is sent to if they click the ad. Similarly house buyers can be segmented into owner occupiers and investors. Owner occupiers into first time buyers, etc. The more specific the campaigns, the ads within the ad groups and keywords associated with these the more effective each is likely to be. The firm will also be able to measure performance with much greater accuracy.

Perhaps the two most important things to bear in mind when it comes to AdWords and pay-per-click generally is control and scale, as PPC is the antithesis of SEO. With SEO you might hit the jackpot and get on the front page, but you really have no way of controlling this and you can't scale it. You might do it once in one area but you may have difficulty maintaining and replicating it when you want to.

With AdWords the situation is entirely reversed. Once you have your campaign set up correctly, you know what you are doing and you are carefully monitoring results, you can tweak a campaign empirically to produce a level of performance that is optimal for you. Then once you have done this experimentally on a pilot basis with a low budget, you can turn up the dial as high as you like and expect performance to increase accordingly.

Bear in mind however that the corollary of this is also true: if you don't set it up correctly, don't know what you are doing and do not monitor results carefully and adjust accordingly as soon as possible you can burn an awful lot of completely wasted cash with AdWords. This is probably where most people have a bad experience and give up. But ultimately this is down to an amateur approach and a failure to appreciate the extent to which it is necessary to invest in experimentation rather than a fundamental problem with the advertising platform. It works once you have campaigns designed to produce measurable results. You must ensure that each campaign is sending traffic to a dedicated landing page on your website so that you can measure results for each campaign separately. Each landing page must provide a compelling offer with a call to action designed to convert the response to that ad into a new Lead on your List. In this way you can track results from your advertising investment in each campaign very clearly. This will tell you where you are getting a positive ROI and where you are not, enabling you to make changes quickly and avoid wasting money on advertising that isn't working.

Bing is Microsoft's answer to Google. It comes pre-installed as the default search engine on many Microsoft products. Google is dominant in the international search engine business with over 66% of market share internationally in 2014. Separate data for Ireland is hard to come by but it looks like Google's dominance of search is well over 90% in Ireland at present. But Bing does have a presence, particularly when you consider how many people use Microsoft products and just go along with whatever is pre-installed on their machines by default.

Bing Ads is Microsoft's answer to Google's AdWords. For our purposes here everything that has been said about AdWords applies to Bing Ads with the obvious exception that the search network on which the ads will be displayed will be Bing's rather than Google's.

Should you consider using Bing Ads? There are a few reasons why you might: first off, while the volumes will be much lower (and in Ireland bear in mind that volumes are relatively small anyway, so you're only going to be getting 5 or 10% of what is a small number to start with) the quality of the traffic can be higher and there are fewer advertisers operating there too. Secondly, because the volumes are small you will not need a big budget to experiment and you will not burn cash at the same rate as you will on AdWords. The downside of this is that you won't get results, or statistically reliable data to measure those results, as quickly. Finally, from an advertiser's perspective Bing tends to be a little more approachable than Google. They need to be competitive and because the platforms are so similar it is very easy to transpose a campaign from one to the other. AdWords is definitely the place the start but don't overlook Bing Ads.

Social Media Advertising

This is essentially PPC advertising also, so much of what we have said in relation to AdWords applies here too.

As with SEO in the case of AdWords, the important thing to remember with social media advertising is that it is *not* social media marketing. You are not out there tweeting, liking, plus oneing or otherwise "engaging" with the world and his wife. Here you are advertising on social media sites. You pay the sites for the rights to have your ads shown there, and there are a variety of ways in which they can appear depending on the platform. The key is that you are paying for a service and in this respect it is in the interest of the sites to provide you with a decent return on that investment to keep you coming back for more. As is the case with paid versus organic traffic generally, your interests as an advertiser on social media sites are much more closely aligned with the site owners than the interests of users, particularly business users, trying to get exposure for free.

There are truly tons of social media sites and as soon as this book goes to press there'll be more that'll probably have eclipsed others. At present, the Daddy is Facebook. You may not like it or use it but an awful lot of other people do. You might also feel that Facebook is not terribly suitable for your practice area, but again bear in mind that the people consuming your services may well spend a lot of their spare time on Facebook and all that matters to them is whether the ad is relevant, not where they see it.

Apart from Facebook, the other huge social phenomenon is Twitter and it is quite a different place to Facebook. If Facebook is where people go to hang out, Twitter is where they go to *find out*. Twitter's big on news; it spreads like wildfire there. I mention Twitter here for the sake of completeness, but from an advertising perspective Twitter's platform is still quite new and developing.

And the third one of particular relevance to Real Lawyers from an advertising standpoint is LinkedIn. LinkedIn has established a dominant position for itself as the social media account of professionals and business. As far as I can see most go on there just to look and see what other professionals in their own field are up to but none the less it is big for this and has a huge network. If you're selling B2B, LinkedIn can have serious potential.

Let's look at the two with most potential for Real Law firms in more detail.

Facebook

Facebook is huge and at the time of writing has something in the region of 1.3 billion active users, being a frightening proportion of the total world population. For some Facebook *is* the internet. Facebook also has something that makes it particularly powerful and unique: it captures an incredible amount of data about the people who use it. They tell Facebook their age, their address, where they went to school, what they do for a living, what their social statuses are, and on and on. And that's even before they start telling Facebook by their activity what they are interested in, etc. What this means is that Facebook has a uniquely powerful ability to target users by reference to key attributes. The extent to which you can harness this is truly awesome.

Facebook advertising has been around for quite a while but as a platform it has really matured and come into its own recently. It's amazing what the drive to make profits will do for a business's ability to get its stuff together.

What you have with Facebook is an unprecedented ability to get your ad in front of a very highly targeted audience and the greater the extent to which you are prepared to narrow the focus of this targeting the greater success you will have with this.

First, let's have a look at the basics. As with the other platforms, it really doesn't make sense to get too hung up on the user interface as it's constantly changing, however in general terms on Facebook viewers have the news feed and the sidebar.

The news feed is the main central scrolling area where all of a Prospective Client's Friends' posts appear. Facebook advertising allows you to publish ads that will appear in the Friends' news feeds as if they had been posted by their own Friends.

Interestingly Facebook advertising has only recently enabled this and previously it was possible for business pages to have posts appearing in the news feeds of those who Liked the page. But Facebook got wise to this and restricted it or stopped it completely, deciding that this was something businesses should have to pay for. Many businesses that had been very successful in using social media marketing for free found themselves unable to do so almost overnight and much moaning and wailing and grinding of teeth ensued. But this is just a classic example of how reliance on free can be disastrous.

The fact that the ads now appear in the news feed is something that users have had to get used to as well. Some don't like it and react badly too it, assuming that the publisher of the ad has placed it before them and is somehow "spamming them". But of course the person publishing the ad has merely submitted it to Facebook, and Facebook is the entity who decided when and where it will place the ad.

The other place in which Facebook ads can appear is on the side bar. This is where ads have more traditionally tended to appear on Facebook and they are more familiar as a result. Users expect to see ads there and know that they are ads; and that's not necessarily a bad thing as we have seen from PPC in other areas. You will find that a buyer clicking on an ad is a far better prospect to come to your website than a searcher who is just browsing through on an organic search result.

Here's an example from my own Facebook page showing an ad in the news feed and on the side bar:

A Facebook page with ads in news feed and side bar.

To advertise on Facebook you need to create an ad for the news feed and an ad for the side bar. Or more (possibly many more) than one of each depending on how you propose to do this.

When creating your ad, think target audience. Well of course, you should always be thinking target audience in any ad, but on Facebook you have so much power and control in terms of who you place the ad in front of it's really worth a bit of effort in making your ad relevant to the particular niche that you propose to target.

This is when you get to the really powerful bit on Facebook. Having created the ad you wish to appear, you are then able to select who you wish your ads to appear in front of. You can choose by location, gender, age, relationship status, occupation, and on and on. It really is possible to be ridiculously specific. As you refine your target audience Facebook will tell you the size of your estimated audience which will shrink as you add each new criterion.

For example, say you choose a target market for a particular family law ad as "married women in Dublin with children under primary school age". Facebook's audience selection tool allows you to choose the age of the people the ad will be shown to; like this:

This audience is very specific and in the example above the ad would only be shown to 5,800 people.

Reducing the size of your target audience in such a selective way is a *good thing*. Counterintuitively, a smaller more highly-qualified audience is almost always more preferable than a larger generic group. Most of the latter are going to be completely uninterested in what you've got to offer, so clicks from these people will be an utter waste and you'll have to pay for them.

The other remarkable thing about Facebook advertising is that the cost of traffic from Facebook is considerably less than that from AdWords. This will be subject to change of course, but it is currently an advertising platform that has really come of age and presents incredible opportunities for the time being.

You may of course take the view that your prospects are not on Facebook, particularly if you're in a B2B market and it may be true that they don't necessarily look for what you're providing on Facebook. But the likelihood is that they probably are on Facebook when they're not at work. If you can present them with an appropriate offer that is targeted very carefully for them (and remember you can do this with great precision) you may find traffic from very serious matters indeed coming from Facebook.

For example, in estate planning services for high net worth individuals you may wish to target people with children who have had matrimonial issues who want to ensure that their grandchildren benefit directly in their estate. Many grandparents use Facebook specifically to keep in contact with their grandkids.

LinkedIn

On many levels LinkedIn advertising is very similar to Facebook advertising. You don't have the same level of granularity in terms of how closely you can segment and target your market but you can go a pretty long way towards it.

The ads on LinkedIn are essentially banner ads that will appear on or around the various screens a Prospective Client might visit. (Banner ads are discussed shortly.) Basically when the Prospective Client logs on to the LinkedIn home screen, views their profile, someone else's profile or their LinkedIn inbox, these banners will be placed at the side, top or bottom. Here's an example from my own LinkedIn page showing a plain text ad at the top and banner ads on the side:

A LinkedIn Home page with ads at the top and on the side.

As with all of these services the first thing you will need to do after you create a campaign is design your ad, which you will do with your specific target market in mind.

Next you will be asked to select the target audience for your ad and this is where the nature of LinkedIn comes in to its own in a B2B setting. People register with LinkedIn for business, to showcase their wares as a professional or business provider. Therefore, they provide details on their educational and professional qualifications, their work experience, locations and so on. Some will have just filled out the bare minimum to create a profile so that they can go on the site and lurk at everyone else in their industry who's on there already. Others will make varying degrees of efforts to create a good impression to their prospects on the site. This information is what LinkedIn will use to decide to whom they might show your ads.

So on LinkedIn the types of criteria that you are going to be able to target will include industry, type of business within an industry, size of organisation, position within the organisation and geographical location. You can also select negative criteria; i.e. criteria which you wish to exclude from your search and not show your ads to.

For instance, say you wanted to target insolvency practitioners. You would start by selecting the location: Ireland. You would then choose a category based on industry and firm size. LinkedIn does not have a separate category for insolvency practitioners but if you are targeting accountants as opposed to lawyers you might choose the finance industry and from that select the accounting category.

You can then narrow it to firm size. You might be targeting practitioners only in large firms or in small ones, you can narrow the search to firms with 1 -10 employees, 11 – 50, 51 -200 and so on up to firms sized 10,000+. If there are specific firms that you wish to target you can include those by name.

You can exclude companies on the same basis. There are many other categories based around skills, qualifications and group association that you can chose to include or exclude from your search criteria.

Paid Online Methods

Again this audience is quite specific and in the example
above the ad would only be shown to 1,206 people.

You can't be as granular with LinkedIn as you can with Facebook. The geographical area for instance is limited to Ireland rather than quite small and specific geographical areas on Facebook but this reflects the size of the network and the number of people on it. However, depending on the size of the industry you are targeting you can really get quite specific indeed in terms of the type, number and quality of people that you are targeting.

With LinkedIn your ad can promote a website or content. In order to be able to track results your ad should be promoting a website. I use the term *website* here because that is what they use on the ad creation tool in LinkedIn. But of course you will not be promoting a website at all. Rather you will be promoting a landing page; i.e. a very specific page on your website where you will be sending traffic from this LinkedIn campaign and only this campaign. This way you will be able to tailor the page's content to be relevant to the people who click the link from the LinkedIn ad.

You will also be able to track results from the ad to identify precisely how your ad is performing.

If you are selling to a B2B market, with a little thought you could develop a highly targeted and potentially very effective campaign on LinkedIn for the right offer to generate Leads from the right kind of Prospective Client. And that's what it's all about at the end of the day.

Banner Ads

Banner ads are the main type of advertising that you see on websites. They are ads that appear as rectangular "banners" around the top, sides and bottom of web pages as you browse them. They are there in your field of vision as an ad might appear on a banner on a hoarding in the physical world. They can be dynamic – the content may change or move – so the possibilities are only limited by one's imagination.

The banner will contain a mixture of text and images to convey your message. The banner itself will generally be one big rectangular button and if anyone clicks on the banner they will be taken to the link that you have assigned to the banner: your landing page for that ad.

I mention banner ads here as a separate category just to cover the expression and to give you the complete picture. In fact banner ads cover everything we've been talking about in Facebook and LinkedIn as the ads that appear there are banner ads.

The difference with sites like Facebook and LinkedIn is that their ads can target audiences very precisely.

On general websites, banner ads can tend to sit there and just be shown to everyone either permanently or in some kind of rotation. Depending on the niche you're in and the market you're targeting, old fashioned simple banner ads with a really good offer for that target market can be really effective. You just need to be realistic in your expectations. A classic example would be a banner ad targeting house buyers for conveyancing services on an auctioneer's website.

Remarketing

Most people encounter this phenomenon unwittingly. They have the experience where they keep seeing the same ad or related ads for the same product or service online. This is remarketing or retargeting.

Remarketing is a particular type of banner ad. Google will display a remarketing ad based on a searcher's browsing history. It involves the use of cookies.

For example, when a person visits a Real Law firm's website and spends time on a conveyancing page, the person's web browser receives cookies from that page which create a record of that visit. The primary function of cookies is to make a user's browsing experience swifter and more seamless. As with everything on the web the trade-off for this is privacy, because cookies track browsing history.

Remarketing uses these cookies to allow Google to show ads based on that browsing history. This way, in the example referred to above, the searcher might suddenly notice that he or she is regularly shown a banner for conveyancing services from the firm whose site they visited previously.

At its most basic, remarketing allows you to show highly targeted ads to someone who has clearly expressed an interest in the subject matter. When an ad is being seen by Prospective Clients who have been to your site already, the ad has a far better chance of producing results. By comparison, an untargeted ad appearing on the Internet may only be seen by people who have never expressed any interest in what you have to offer. Following the principle of the moving parade, as the Prospective Client's parade of interest moves along, if your ad appears at a point in time when they are more interested in what you've got to offer or more inclined to act upon it, your ad will be likely to have a much higher chance of success than it might have had at any other time.

To get the full benefit of remarketing you need to use it systematically. Just showing the person the same banner ad such as one that might appear cold on a completely new search for keywords associated with that topic is better than nothing. However, this doesn't use the medium to its full potential. To really harness the power of this technology that visitor could be shown an ad that speaks directly about the content of the page that they previously visited. The ad does not have to start from scratch, so the ad copy can be refined to present something more relevant to this person. This will not be suitable in all practice areas or in all cases, but there are many areas in which it can be a useful, effective and appropriate way of presenting something that has previously been rejected or ignored to a prospect in a slightly different way. For instance, if someone visited a page on your site where a hard copy guide was offered to be sent to them in the post but they did not take up the offer, the remarketing ad might direct them back to a different page where an electronic copy is available for immediate download instead.

Paid Online Methods

Note about cookies: you have to ensure that visitors to your site are aware of the fact that your site uses cookies (if it does). Your privacy policies have to make it clear exactly to what use cookies may be put and you should obtain consent to their use. If you have a website you need to ensure that you are fully compliant with the electronic marketing regulations (which are reviewed in more detail in Appendix 2) whether you use services like remarketing or not.

> ➤ Develop targeted campaigns in PPC advertising for specific services sending clicks to dedicated landing pages.
> ➤ AdWords is controllable and scalable, unlike SEO.
> ➤ PPC advertising on social media is different from social media marketing in the same way.
> ➤ Facebook: enormous user base with incredible targeting opportunities to create extremely focussed campaigns. B2C rather than B2B.
> ➤ LinkedIn: smaller user base but highly targeted at professionals and business. Entirely B2B. Good targeting based on industries, size of organisation and position.
> ➤ Remarketing is a powerful tool to augment basic PPC campaigns.

Chapter 17: Print Media

Half the money I spend on advertising is wasted; the trouble is, I don't know which half.

– John Wanamaker

In your Real Law firm toolkit you have both online and offline tools. The best strategy to promote your firm will be to combine both types of tools, utilising the strengths of each.

Your efforts to drive traffic to your website should not be exclusively focussed on online methods. Offline sources of traffic can be equally, if not more, effective once used correctly. In this model you might think of it as a two-step process where you're using an offline medium to get the Prospective Client online to make the connection, after which you take them offline again to follow up.

As covered earlier, your website is the hub; you use the power of the Internet to make the connection or to enable responses but you do not use it to the exclusion of other more traditional tools. The new Internet tool can breathe fresh life into the older offline tools. Each is a part of a business development system in which they are far more powerful and effective together than any could be on its own.

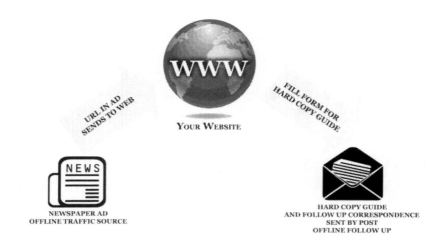

URL IN AD SENDS TO WEB

FILL FORM FOR HARD COPY GUIDE

YOUR WEBSITE

NEWSPAPER AD
OFFLINE TRAFFIC SOURCE

HARD COPY GUIDE
AND FOLLOW UP CORRESPONDENCE
SENT BY POST
OFFLINE FOLLOW UP

Traffic Can Go Online from Offline Sources
And back Offline again for Follow Up

Most solicitors' print ads are dreadful; even the fancy ones done by expensive ad agencies. They tend to make one of two fundamental mistakes: they either talk all about the solicitor's practice, their skill, experience, results and level of service or they go with some esoteric brand building gobbledegook that no-one understands but everyone in the office loves because it's cool and sophisticated or funny. Or failing either of those they have the classic in the small local firm in particular where they get buttonholed to take an ad in support of the local good cause at the last minute where they just end up with something saying, "Proudly supporting Clonakilty Primary School; McCarthy & Co. for all your legal needs"[3].

The principles of print advertising are exactly the same as all of the others online and offline. You need to think *direct response*

---

[3] I've been there and bought that particular T-shirt in my time; believe me. But there is a better way. Read on.

and you need to work from a number of very simple and unsexy basic principles.

The most important of those principles is the AIDA formula: Attention, Interest, Desire and Action. It is simple and universal; as long as your Prospective Clients are human beings from planet Earth the AIDA formula will work for you in creating ad copy. You can spend practically as much as you wish on fancy ad copywriters or on learning how to write brilliant ad copy, but at its core it all comes down to this.

First you need to get the Prospective Client's Attention. You need a headline that does this for you. And remember the purpose of the headline is not to sell the product or service; it is to get their attention so that they read the rest of the ad.

Then you need to get the Prospective Client Interested. This is the ad copy. You need to set out in engaging language why on Earth the person reading the ad should look at what you are offering.

Then you need to create Desire. We're not necessarily talking chocolates and flowers here but rather you have to get the Prospective Client to want what it is that you are offering.

And finally you have to get the Prospective Client to take Action. Every ad must have a clear call to action that motivates the reader to take the next step. The call to action could simply to be to contact you. But as covered in the Lead Generation model, a more effective call to action might be that the Prospective Client is urged to avail of an offer of information which flows through to a follow-up sequence designed to lead them more gradually to that initial contact.

If you're using print ads as a means of driving traffic to your landing page, the call to action will be a web address to which you are directing the reader.

While you should have only one offer that you are trying to make with the ad, you should provide multiple ways to respond. The reader could be invited to visit a site, call a number, email or write to you.

Again it is whatever is going to be most convenient for your target market that will determine what works best. It is down to what suits and works best for them not what you want and the only way you're ever going to really find out what does and doesn't work is by asking the market, by taking out ads and testing them.

Where should you place print ads? This is among the last questions you should be asking. It only becomes relevant or open for consideration after the following 5 steps:

1. Who do you want to attract? Identify your Ideal Client.

2. What are the problems that they are trying to solve? *It's not about you*, it's about them and what matters to them may not be what you think. Find out by asking them.

3. How can you get them to identify themselves to you (i.e. raise their hands by showing their interest, usually by requesting some easy accessible information)? Then you can tailor follow-up just for them.

4. If they don't make an appointment immediately, then what can you do to keep them interested in you until they are ready to make a decision to make an appointment with a lawyer?

5. Even after they make the decision to go with you, what follow-up sequences are you going to have in place to reinforce their idea to hire you?

Step 6 is the media question and you only come to ask it after you have taken steps 1 to 5.

6. How can you get in front of where your Ideal Client may be looking when they're thinking, "Maybe I need a solicitor?"

Most people get this ass backwards. They want to start with, "Where should we place our ad or spend our marketing euros?" However, it is very important to be crystal clear on the answers to the questions at 1 to 5 first.

But let's say you've gone through this exercise and you feel print ads may be worth testing; again think *testing*. Don't assume that the first ad you're going to take out is going to get the phone ringing or because it doesn't that it's a waste. Each ad is an experiment to be tested against all previous versions, the best of which you call *the control*. The object of the exercise in any direct response campaign is to continually try to beat the control, changing one (and only one) thing at a time. This is why direct response as a concept is so vital. Unless you have people taking action in response to your ads which you can measure and compare against previous and future performance you have no way of making any rational assessment of whether any particular ad is working and whether in doing so it is working better or worse than the control.

Finally, as well as testing you must think tracking. A direct response to your advertising is what you are after and in order to be able to measure your response you have to be able to track it.

You can track this manually to some extent by asking people where they heard about you when they call but this can be patchy and if someone does get in contact about a serious issue that is important to them, you may not wish to introduce distractions to that first conversation by quizzing the person on how they heard about you. The answer is to build tracking in to your calls to action. Use a dedicated number in your ad and make sure that you can track calls from that number so that you can identify which calls coming in to your office are coming from that ad. If you have a web address in your ad as a means of response (which you should), don't use your home page. Create a dedicated landing page for the ad and use a dedicated web address (a uniform resource locator or URL) pointing to that page in your ad. You need to know what works and how well and what doesn't work at all and you won't be able to, unless you can measure response effectively by tracking it.

Let's take a look at some specifics:

Local Press and Free Papers

Local press usually typified by the regional weeklies up and down the country are great papers and they really get read. *Everyone* reads the local weekly in our area. It comes out on a Thursday morning and by Thursday lunchtime those in the know will have the latest on who's in the paper. It covers local news, sport and colour and for that reason it gets read and read more than once, each copy going through a number of hands.

Ads done well in this type of publication can be really effective. But beware! Beware of the approach from the local paper to run an ad as part of a special feature or in support of some other local venture. This is usually a complete waste of time and will just place you with an ad or advertorial saying something utterly banal, often in the company of one or more of your competitors.

If you are going to advertise in local press do so on your terms for very specific, strategic reasons. Do not end up advertising there by default because the local rep just happens to twist your arm and tells you what a great idea it is and how well it's worked for your competitors. And do not let the rep who sold you on the idea of advertising create the copy and design for your ad. This is often part of the sales pitch: they've got a great design team who really know their onions on this advertising lark, and they'll produce an ad you'll love. Well, yes, you may look at it and think it makes you look great, but from a direct response point of view it may be as effective as a chocolate teapot; lovely to look at and all that.

Similarly there are many excellent local free papers now of an almost endless number of hues and varieties. These have great potential too. Like the local paid press they pass through many hands and depending on the frequency of publication and how well they're done, each issue may have surprising longevity. There's a free monthly in our area that seems to have an extraordinary reach because it passes through a great many hands and remains relevant and read over the entire month that it's in circulation. The right local ad there can be tremendously effective.

Again this all comes down to the 5 step process above that you must go through before you consider your medium. Do a little thinking on this and you can really get results.

The first thing you should do is research them. Buy or pick up copies of the papers in your target locality and read them. See who advertises there. (You'll notice that the Injuries Board advertises in local regional papers quite regularly.) See who they're aimed at. Does this align with your target market? Are there sections or topics covered that are likely to be particularly relevant to your target market? Work from there. You can often advertise at very modest rates in these papers and the paper is being read so you can be sure the right ad will be seen. Because you can advertise affordably here it is an ideal medium for testing and refining ad copy.

Specialist and Trade Press

This is definitely niche but by now you know that niche is where you want to be. It's probably more relevant for B2B but not necessarily. For example, there have been a variety of judicial review applications relating to firearms legislation and at least one firm of solicitors has placed long copy ads in a shooting magazine inviting those who might be affected by a particular issue to contact it. I'm sure you can appreciate that the right ad on this topic placed in a magazine dedicated to shooting enthusiasts is going to be appearing before a very highly qualified target[4] audience who are buying that publication because they have an interest in the very topic you're talking about in the first place. How this might cross over between practice areas on a B2C level requires a little thought and imagination; are gardeners, anglers, car enthusiasts, history buffs more likely to have an interest in a

---

[4] Excuse the pun.

particular practice area? Do a little research on the demographics each magazine aims at; there could be very interesting crossovers with the demographics you are trying to reach. For instance, gardening magazines might well provide a good target audience for estate planning ads.

In the B2B area this is much more obvious and direct. If you're targeting accountants start with Accountancy Ireland, for the fishing industry try Marine Times, for farmers it's the Farmer's Journal. And of course you can get far more sophisticated and targeted than this focussing on niches within specific sectors, with a little imagination.

The thing to remember is that your ad in these publications must follow the AIDA principles already covered. The ad has to speak to your Ideal Client in their own language and provide something that will get their Attention, to develop an Interest and lead to a Desire which will spur them to Action.

National Press

This is the big league; championship hurling. Definitely not for the faint-hearted. That's not to say don't do it; just make sure you know what you're doing. Use tried and tested copy and be ruthless about results. Apart from entering the racehorse business the best way to make a small fortune is to start with a big fortune and start brand advertising in the national press. The Sunday papers are particularly adept at this and will hit you up every so often with the prospect of a feature on your region, your industry, the award you've just won or whatever that you can't afford to miss. If it fits all of your other criteria it may be worth considering, just don't be tempted because everyone else is doing it so you won't be left out.

The last place you want to be in this business is in a fancy feature with your direct competitors while you're paying for the privilege.

Golden Pages

The print version of the Golden Pages is undeniably a medium that has suffered decline in recent years. Certainly, the book is now a fraction of the thickness it used to be.

That in itself may provide an opportunity to advertise there. The fact that advertisers are moving elsewhere means less competition in this medium than there used to be and you may be able to negotiate significant reductions in rates. Presumably it is still being used by an older demographic and you may find it worth experimenting with for practice areas an older readership might be in the market for: wills, enduring powers of attorney, etc.

The difficulty with this option is that it requires a reasonably substantial annual commitment in what is at this stage a speculative and declining medium. And those that have strong established positions there are likely to continue with big defensive ads for as long as it continues to work for them.

For instance, recently they introduced a fold out tab on a heavy card first page of the "solicitors" section of the book. The thing stands out a mile. Whoever gets that tab (and presumably is paying most in the book as a result), is probably hoovering up the vast majority of Golden Pages readers.

So, my take on the Golden Pages is that unless you are willing to go in really big with tested ad copy to take on those that already have established dominant positions there, it's going to be difficult to get a return better than you can get more easily elsewhere. The real question is whether you can take advantage of its recent decline in popularity with other advertisers.

- ➢ Use print media in conjunction with online.
- ➢ Always use the AIDA formula in creating content: Attention, Interest, Desire and Action.
- ➢ Your ad must always have a call to *action*.
- ➢ Test everything and track response.
- ➢ Use local press and free papers for local business; widely read with multiple readership. Cost effective way of testing ads.
- ➢ Use specialist press to target niche areas. Think how demographics might overlap.
- ➢ Only go national when you know what you are doing with copy you have tested.

Chapter 18: Other Traffic Sources

Some are born great, some achieve greatness, and some hire public relations officers.

– Daniel J. Boorstin

Direct Mail

Direct mail is one of the oldest forms of marketing: the sending of letters, postcards or packages with any combination of enclosures to individuals in the post. It is a bit of a blind spot for many who never think of it as a modern form of marketing but that is a grave error. As I mentioned in Chapter 8, firms like Google use direct mail extensively. And if savvy Internet giants are using direct mail, you can be sure that there is nothing old fashioned about it; direct mail works.

It makes a lot of sense when you think about it: we are bombarded by electronic communications and interruption messages. Emails, tweets and posts flow over us all day every day and advertisements come from every angle through TV, radio, the Internet, our physical environment, you name it. So we are inclined to switch off and to ignore and forget about an awful lot of what we encounter. Email is particularly prone to this; it is ignored or deleted unread wholesale, if it ever actually makes it into the inbox at all.

But direct mail is different. Think about the actual mail you receive on a regular basis. Most of it comprises bills and statements and other generally unwelcome or unexciting items. A personal note or card is a real highlight and can make a big difference to your day.

Most importantly, the point at which someone receives direct mail – at the end of their hallway when they bend down to pick up the post from the floor – is a point in time at which they are likely to have relatively few distractions. Their day is over or may not yet have begun, they may well be alone and they do not have a million other messages or distractions flashing across their screen.

At that moment you have a unique opportunity to get the person's undivided attention if your piece of direct mail is suitably interesting, useful or helpful to them.

Perhaps two reasons why direct mail is out of vogue are very practical: it costs money and takes a bit of effort. You've got to create copy, proofread it, print material, place it in envelopes and pay for its delivery. Email is much easier and cheaper. But what would you rather send: a cheap and easy email that never gets delivered, opened or read or something that actually gets results? Again, think about ROI and not just the price here.

One key to success with direct mail is the quality and segmentation of the List to which it is sent. Bear in mind of course that, as with everything else, you must comply with Advertising Regulations and Data Protection requirements in the compilation and selection of the mailing List.

Once you have a List of the right recipients for your message, the next most important thing is to make sure that it gets delivered. Don't take this for granted and take a bit of care with the quality of what you are sending on the outside of the envelope. This is the first thing that anyone handling the piece will see and it will determine their attitude to it. You don't want it to look like a circular or it might never make it into the letterbox. Similarly on open rates: what it looks like from the outside will make a huge difference. You have to weigh practicality against results here: the more effort you put in and the more personal you can make it, the better your results can be.

You have to decide on the balance you strike: for instance a real stamp and a handwritten address on a good quality envelope has a much higher likelihood of being delivered and opened than one that has been clearly sent in bulk.

After that, the principles governing your content on the inside are exactly the same as those applying to every other message we have discussed throughout the book, particularly the AIDA formula.

PR

PR is a dark art; or at least PR people would like you to think so. A lot of it seems to be about relationships and I suspect that PR people spend a lot of time building relationships with the right people in the right places in the media. If you're a journalist, an editor or a producer and you want something you know is going to work when it's important, the recommendation of someone you trust is probably always going to trump any other source.

But even well-connected PR people have to produce good stories and that is something you're just as well able to do as anyone. But again you need to think like a consumer of this material. And you need to think that your initial consumer is not the news-consuming public but the journalists, editors and producers who create the news. You need to think in terms of material that is going to be interesting and useful to them and how they can use that for their public. You need to think first of all in terms of newsworthiness. Journalists and editors are always looking for good material on deadlines. If there is a particular story in the news, related stories around that will be very attractive to them. Think of how your area of specialism might be able to contribute to a story in the news. Do you have a unique take on it or an experience or angle that might shed a whole new light on the story? It's really all about using a little imagination.

As with advertising, the best place to start is with your local media outlets. They're always looking for news and good stories are not always that thick on the ground. But don't come to this from the point of view of "How can I get my name in the paper?"; rather think "How can I provide them with good content that will make their story better?" *It's not about you*, it's about them and their audience; sound familiar?

Social media is particularly useful for getting in contact with journalists. Twitter is especially good for this. Journalists scan Twitter as it is the fastest vector for breaking news. By using Twitter you can get a feel for what journalists are interested in and the stories they are following. I'm not talking about being creepy and stalking people here, but by using Twitter as it is intended to be used, you can get a feel for what is going on. Once you find your voice on the medium you can start to get to know people and build relationships. This takes time and a bit of effort, but it can be very worthwhile. If you see someone looking for information or resources on Twitter or answers to questions that you are easily able to provide, jump in and be helpful. Don't expect instant results but once you've developed a reputation as someone who knows what you're talking about, is reliable, helpful and quick, you're well on the way to building that relationship that makes you a good source of information. You can build on this by providing stories or background to stories based on your particular area of expertise and experience.

Sometimes when it comes to PR I hear people say that journalists are lazy and if you write the story for them they'll just cut and paste it. Well that's not my experience. I don't think journalists are lazy any more than solicitors, teachers or farmers are lazy; sure there are lazy examples of each but none more so than in any other group. But journalists are *busy*, working to tight deadlines in a 24/7 fast-paced news cycle.

So you have to think in terms of material that is helpful and relevant to them. Cut to the chase; explain things in terms that will be relevant to their audience. Understand the nature of the news world within which they live and work. Always find out what their deadlines are and respect them; never leave them hanging. Develop trust and mutual respect.

Apart from that, every now and then you need to get lucky. But as the saying goes, the harder you work the luckier you get. You need to keep working on the quality of the material that you can contribute and keep building relationships, then when stories appear in the news on which you have something to say, you have to jump on them. This is one situation in which you cannot sit back; timing is critical here. Nothing may come of it and what you put out there may fall on fallow ground. You can't expect everything you put out to get on the front page. But if you keep at it, you will find that you can establish a reputation and if you keep showing up in a timely fashion whenever stories that you can provide expert commentary on are in the news you will find it easier and easier for your voice to be heard.

Networking

Networking may seem like a funny one to have on a list of ways to generate traffic, but it's important that you think of it as just another one. Don't think just about online activity like SEO, pay-per-click or whatever, or even traditional methods like offline paid advertising driving traffic to your site; instead think of everything you do as part of a direct response marketing strategy. The same goes for your customer service driving referrals and the way you greet new people when they walk in the door.

And so networking can be as good a way to drive traffic to your business as any, depending on the practice area to some extent.

But be careful about networking; as with social media, you can spend an awful lot of time "networking" that can turn out to be an unproductive waste of your time unless you are clear on your objectives and have a plan.

Before you consider any kind of networking, decide what you want to achieve from it. What kind of business do you want to get from it, are you looking for people who can refer work to you from others or are you looking to get business directly. Perhaps it's both. Whatever it is your whole approach should be driven by what you want to make happen.

Then think about how you are going to make this happen, once you have identified your target audience and the type of business or referral you might get from them, what action are you going to want them to take? Do you have anything that you can offer that will make this easy or enticing for them? How can you help them to do whatever it is that moves them in the direction you need towards the business that you want?

In this way you can see networking to be just another type of traffic generation activity. You might provide people with information, material or an offer that drives them towards calling a number, visiting a site or returning a post card. In this respect the concept of a call to action is no different to any other message, the only difference being that this one is delivered personally, by you.

Next, don't go out there desperately looking for business or referrals. The best metaphor I have heard is that your network is like a fruit tree. You can't go out there one day, plant a tree and expect fruit from it next week. It takes time and in the meantime you have to feed and nurture the network before it will bear fruit. And if you neglect a fruit tree, even after you think you have it to maturity, you will experience very poor yields of mediocre fruit.

So if networking works for your practice area use it, but use it like any other traffic generation method, think target audience, most desired action, offer designed to achieve that and call to action. Then think strategically and give your network sufficient time, care and attention to start bearing fruit.

Publishing

You are holding in your hands the best business card in the world. Books are incredibly powerful in our culture. It's no co-incidence that the top expert in the field is referred to as the "guy who wrote the book on it". Writing a book gives you expert status almost automatically. Books are also very durable. People don't throw books away, even bad ones. A business card or brochure may go in the bin but a book tends to stick around. The destruction of books is synonymous with oppressive regimes, think book burning in Nazi Germany, and therefore, we are, as a culture, slow to destroy or otherwise dispose of books; the worst fate often being to pass it on to someone else.

For these reasons writing a book can be one of the most powerful things you can do in positioning yourself as an expert to your target market and in providing yourself with one of the best Lead Generation offers you can make. You really should write a book.

But, you say, "I can't write a book, I don't have time." Well, you do; you have the same amount of time as everyone else, it's just a question of how you spend it. I wrote this book over a number of months while working full time. I blocked time when I left the office and went to a remote location for a number of hours each day once I had the essentials covered in the office each morning and I'd come back later in the afternoon to tidy up anything that needed to get out before the end of the day. I told people where I was, which was a short walk from our office. I didn't take a mobile and I didn't have WIFI where I went. If there was a life or death situation someone could physically walk over and get me but otherwise I just wasn't contactable. It is amazing what you can get done when you don't have phones and email present in your personal space. You should do it more often for everything even if you never thought of writing a book.

And bear in mind that your book does not need to be a heavy weight technical tome, in fact it shouldn't be. It should explain what you do for your target market in terms that they can understand. In fact you need to work very hard to avoid the type of legal writing that comes naturally to lawyers and write for non-lawyers.

This ties in perfectly with the type of content you need for your blog. You can repurpose content from your blog to provide the content for your book. Use your blog to write your book in instalments by thinking strategically and plan your blog content in advance.

Writing a book is one of the most powerful things you can do to fast-track yourself to expert status, it provides you with a very valuable tool in your marketing and is something that you can do with a little bit of discipline and organisation.

How do you go about it? Well, there are two main routes; published or self-published.

1. Published:

This involves finding a publisher that you can interest with your book proposal. Publishing a book through the traditional publishing house route probably adds considerable weight in certain quarters; legal text books for instance. (Though what about the two most important legal texts that almost every solicitor that has ever practised in Ireland will have come across at some stage – Mongey on Probate and Woods' series on District Court and licensing? Both initially self-published.)

However, the status that you may obtain from going the published route comes at a cost. If you go with a traditional publisher, they will own the book. You will get recognition as the author of course but they will have control over print runs, pricing, format and use of content. If you want to give away copies you will have to buy them from the publisher (at a discount, but not a massive one). Future editions and reprints will be at the publisher's discretion.

If you've got a book that's likely to be a popular hit or high in demand or on a topic that publishers are going to be keen on, there may be merit in going this route for the status it brings (but don't be under any illusions about the advance and the launch party you're going to get). Otherwise, it seems to me that for the purposes we are talking about here the self-published route has far more advantages.

2. Self-Published:

If you want to get under the skin of someone who has self-published, call it vanity publishing. Traditionally self-publishing was looked down upon as a route used by the idle rich to get otherwise unworthy or self-indulgent works into print. But like many other things, the world has moved on since this concept was first floated.

In many creative fields – writing, music, cinema, the visual arts – more and more artists are moving away from the control of big business to putting their work out there themselves. While I don't pretend we are creating art for the purposes of what we want to do here by the same token very many similarities exist.

First of all the technologies and services have now developed that enable you to do it yourself quite easily. Even if you don't want to do every bit yourself there are a great many service providers out there that will do as much or as little of the job for you depending on how much input you wish to have. You just have to create the content (and there are even services that will help you with that).

Secondly, self-publishing gives you complete ownership and control of your work. If you want to give away a copy, offer it at a special price or use it in any way as part of a promotion you can do so without anyone else's say so. This is really important for what we are talking about here. If you want to create second editions, special editions, multi-media versions you can do all that and the content is all yours to re-purpose in any way you like.

So, to my mind, the advantages of the self-publishing route in this context far outweigh going the traditional publishing route (and that's without even considering the question of whether anyone else would be willing to publish a book on your topic in the first place).

But however you do, getting into print is one of the smartest things you can do. You might think that it's a huge task and is going to take too long, but whenever you do start, you're probably going to regret that it wasn't today.

TV and Radio

Apart from UK personal injury firms advertising on satellite TV shown here, TV is not a medium that Irish lawyers have embraced. It requires serious budget and commitment. Of course that in itself presents an opportunity. To work from first principles, as with any other medium, you will only know if it is going to be effective for you if you test it once you are clear on your message and who you want to reach with that. If you can afford to test TV, you might want to consider it, though Real Law firms can probably get far better bang for their marketing buck elsewhere without the uncertainty.

However, someone is going to take this space sooner or later and if you're sufficiently confident it might as well be you. TV is a specialist activity requiring expert help, just make sure that the expert understands direct response and don't waste money on brand advertising. If you've got a short slot, don't spent valuable seconds talking about you; think Attention, Interest, Desire and Action. In fact you probably won't have much time to develop interest or desire in a short TV ad so you're probably better off thinking of the ad itself as a *headline-plus-call-to-action*. You want to get the viewer's attention and give them a good reason to take action to call a tracking number or go to a dedicated URL where they can get more information which will do the hard work on the interest and desire. Remember too that in the short attention span of TV land anything you utter should be direct and memorable, especially your phone number and URL.

Radio, particularly local radio, is far more widely used here. And the budget required to test it is far more manageable. Similar considerations apply to those relating to TV with the obvious difference that one is video and the other is audio. Just think that while on TV you can display a number or a URL and the viewer is most likely to be sitting down possibly with a smart phone or a tablet to hand, on radio you're working solely by ear. The listener is probably doing something around the house or at work or driving their car. They're not going to be able to write it down or type it into their phone straight away, so here your call to action has to go straight into their head and stick.

When it comes to radio you've also got to think about your target audience, as specialist stations appeal to particular niches. Obviously local stations will target a geographic area, but various national stations will target different demographics. Think carefully about this in terms of where you chose to put out your message. Don't just go with what you listen to; think about what your Prospective Clients are likely to be listening to.

When TV came along they thought radio was dead. It didn't die and it's a very good example of precisely why we shouldn't ignore older media because newer ones have come along in the meantime. However, there is a new threat to radio and it's podcasting. Podcasting allows anyone to create a channel for audio that can be put out via the Internet. You can find podcasts on whatever interests you online and instead of having to listen to the local radio station available in your area, you can listen to a podcast stream from anywhere in the world via your smartphone or tablet and via a Bluetooth connection in your car as you drive. The thing is that anyone can podcast. It's cheap and easy; podcasting is to radio what YouTube is to TV. It's still emerging in terms of the mass Irish market but it's likely to contain tremendous opportunity. In fact, the real opportunity with podcasting is probably that it doesn't require a mass local market at all but rather can be used to create specialist channels targeting extremely esoteric niches. The bottom line is whether your

Prospective Clients are listening; and if they aren't right now they probably will be sooner or later.

> ➤ Use direct mail, it is still highly effective. It is physical and personal without all of the distractions we have from electronic media.
>
> ➤ In your PR think about what will be interesting and helpful to journalists and their audience.
>
> ➤ Use networking in a planned and focussed way. Set objectives and be clear on how you wish to use networking to achieve them. Give it sufficient time.
>
> ➤ Use a book as the ultimate positioning tool. Don't write technical stuff for lawyers; write accessible information for Prospective Clients.
>
> ➤ On TV and radio get to the point fast. Use a slot to get attention and drive a call to action to a phone number or a URL. Make sure it's short, direct and memorable.

Part IV

Building It Out

There is a lot to get done, but you don't have to do it all at once and, if you are clever, everything that you do will add incrementally to what you have done before. You'll get there one step at a time.

But you need to take the first step and it can seem at times that you are far too busy practising law to be able to spend all of the time that must be required in doing all of this extra stuff.

But if you want to create a properly functioning business you have to start with that first step; remember, *your thing* that you are best at is only one of the three main operational components that you need to give you the sustainable business and the sanity that will enable you to live the life you want.

Part IV provides you with techniques that you can use to start going to work harder *on* your business than you do *in* your business.

Chapter 19: Create Your Vision, Set Your Goals and Take Action

The greater danger for most of us lies not in aiming too high and falling short; but in setting our aim too low, and reaching our mark.

– Michelangelo

This is big picture stuff and it all really starts with why you are doing any of this in the first place. You need to get crystal clear on this. It's going to be essential to motivate you and to enable you to persevere when you need to.

Start with a picture of what you want: a vision you have for yourself or for your family, somewhere you want to live, a lifestyle you want to have. It could be a car or a boat or a holiday home. Perhaps you want to be debt free or financially independent by 50. It could be having the time you want to spend with your kids before they grow up. You might want to be a certain weight or be able to run a marathon. You might want to be able to spend more time on charitable work that is important to you. Dig as deeply as you can when you do this. Figure out your ultimate *why*:

- Why do you want the house or the bank balance or the time? Picture what you will do with it. Make the picture as vivid and detailed as possible: that's your vision.

- And how do think that will make you feel? That's your why.

That feeling the vision gives you is your *why*. Visualise your life the way you want it. Whatever it is, all that matters is that it is something that is really important to you and makes you feel the way you want to. Picture yourself having realised it, describe it to yourself in as much detail as you can and write that down. Go back and review the written description regularly to maintain and develop the image in your mind.

Your vision may be tangible and measurable, but it need not be. The things that will lead to the realisation of your vision will be the progressive achievement of your goals. And whatever about your vision, your goals must be specific and measurable and must have a deadline in time. Your goals should challenge you and you will face obstacles in achieving your goals. When you are stuck on those challenges and obstacles, on the bad days when it looks like you're not going to reach them and it's not worth the effort to try, it is your vision that will give you the motivation to stick with it.

So, next you need to set goals. These can be personal or business goals; indeed both will interact with one another. One of your personal goals might be to have achieved a certain income from your business and one of your business goals might be to free up more time to spend doing things with your family. Don't worry about what categories the goals fall into for now; the important thing is that you set them. For instance, losing weight or getting fit may be personal goals, but doing either of these things is likely to make a significant positive contribution to your business goals as the activities that lead to tangible improvements in personal health and fitness are like gateway habits: they get you moving and provide positive feedback that demonstrates what can be achieved by setting goals and working steadily toward them. These good habits in one area of your life can then transfer easily to others.

Your goals should pose a challenge. The temptation might be to set modest goals that you can accomplish easily, but that's a mistake. The most common regret you hear from those who have had success with goal setting is that they wished they had set more ambitious goals in the first place. Depending on how challenging you make them for yourself or where you find yourself starting from, there will be days on which the goal seems unrealistic or unachievable and you feel like giving up.

A number of different acronyms have been used in the context of setting goals. SMART refers to goals that are Specific, Measurable, Assignable, Realistic and Time-based. Certainly your goals should be specific, measurable and time-based and if you are setting goals for an organisation, individual goals should be assignable to someone who will be responsible for the work required to achieve the goal.

But realistic? You don't want to delude yourself obviously, but you don't want to be too conservative in this context either. Your goals should be sufficiently ambitious and challenging to ensure that you realise your vision. And in order to do so you may need to take your business to an entirely new level, which might be completely unrealistic in the eyes of many, given where you're starting from.

Once you have set goals you must *write them down*. These may be the most important words in this chapter if not this book.

Clear written goals set to a deadline are incredibly powerful, but they must be written down.

Remember this does not have to be perfect or world changing. Just get started, make space in your calendar for some undisturbed time alone, think about where you need to go to get what you want and write down the goals you'll need to accomplish to get there. This isn't a once-off, set-and-forget, exercise. Go back to your goals and review them regularly. Measure how you are doing in your progress towards them by the deadlines you have set for yourself. You can add to, improve on and refine your goals as you become clearer in how you are going about achieving them.

Set interim goals too; you may have big picture, headline, long-term goals that you want to achieve in life and in business over say 5 or 10 years. Set interim goals for 3 years, 1 year and 3 months from now; all building towards your long-term goals and each with its own individual deadline in the meantime

Finally on goal setting, check if any of your goals conflict with one another. Being able to take time out of your business in the short term may conflict with your ability to grow it to the level you need to give you the financial independence you desire in the long term. Where conflicts arise you will have to make a choice based on what is most important in order to realise your vision.

Now that you have goals you need to act. Nothing happens without action and implementation; without these, goals are just pipe dreams. And in order to act effectively you need to plan and prepare. First create an action plan: break down the steps required to attain your goal down into human-sized steps that you are going to be able to accomplish one at a time. Next identify *who* and *what* you need to have in place for each step and what you need to do in order to provide this. Then get moving.

Say for example you set yourself a goal to reach a turnover of €500,000 in divorce litigation within three years. And let's say you target divorce files generating fees of at least €5,000 which you know have a lifetime of approximately 2 years. To have €500,000 in turnover in three years' time, you will have to have 100 files by that deadline. Therefore you will have to have 100 files opened within one year to give you 100 files maturing in the two years after that. So, over the next twelve months you know you need to open 100 files, just over 8 each month. Now you've got a 3-year goal of €500,000, a 1 year goal of 100 new files and a 3-month goal of 25 new files. Then each week you can measure exactly how you are doing in terms of achieving your 3-monthly goal.

And to get headed in the direction of that goal you need to focus on what you get done every day next week. And every hour of that day. And every minute of that hour.

Time is one of the most valuable assets that you possess. The present. Right now. You can't save it or stockpile it and this moment once gone will be gone forever.

Therefore, how you use time and what you get done in the time you make available for your business (time which of course you take from the other things in your life, like your family) is probably the most critical factor in your success.

So, you need to focus on that time and what you get done in it, to the ruthless exclusion of all else.

Time management isn't about getting through all of the things that are screaming at you to be done all day; that's utterly meaningless if many of those things don't need to be done in the first place or should not be done by you.

Therefore, the first thing you need to do is prioritise. Then eliminate interruption to enable you to focus exclusively and unmercifully on the top priority tasks until they are done.

To get started, list all of the things you need to do. All of them. Take some time on this. There may be *a lot*. Don't worry about that. Get them all down no matter how trivial or how long you've been meaning to get around to doing them.

Now prioritise them. Assign them A, B and C status in order of importance. Take a step back while you do this and think in terms of those earlier goals. What are the most important things that need to be done by you to get you to those goals? These are the A tasks. They may not be (and very likely aren't) what you feel are the most pressing tasks or the ones screaming loudest to be done; that's a really important realisation to make.

Once you've identified the A tasks, you may discover more A tasks as part of that process.

For instance engaging in this exercise and setting or reviewing your goals in the first place is an A task. You may not have done before or for a while. By its nature it's the most important thing you can ever do.

A second A task that you may not have thought about previously might be to develop systems and procedures to enable you to have others do B tasks for you effectively. This may take time to set up properly so that you can depend on it, but taking the time to set this up will increase the long-term effectiveness of your time exponentially.

This brings us nicely to B tasks, these are things that need to get done by someone but aren't going to have the same impact on achievement of your goals as your A tasks. Ideally these are tasks you're going to either attend to after the A tasks have been taken care of or have someone else do them for you. If you don't have someone in place who can do these for you, you should make it an A task to find someone. There may be someone else in the firm who can help, you may need to employ someone or you may be able to outsource the task.

B tasks may be very important in terms of the things that need to get done in the office. For instance, issuing proceedings on a matter and dealing with file correspondence are critically important tasks in the legal work of the firm but are B tasks in terms of how any individual file contributes to your overall progress towards your goals.

The C tasks will just have to wait until you have all As and Bs underway satisfactorily.

In fact, it is interesting to see what happens when most Cs just don't get done at all; absolutely nothing most of the time. They don't make any difference to anyone either way. *But keep 'em on the list* for now so that mentally you know where they are in the order of priorities: you haven't completely ignored them you just have more important things that you have to get done first.

Stephen Covey categorised tasks into four quadrants: urgent/important; important/not urgent; urgent/not important; and not urgent/not important.

The Four Quadrants

Essentially the top two quadrants are good, the bottom two bad. The top two quadrants contain important tasks, urgent and non-urgent. The bottom two contain unimportant tasks, again urgent and non-urgent. Time spent in the fourth quadrant is the worst from a productivity point of view, spending time on non-urgent unimportant tasks. You should never be spending work time in this quadrant.

Urgent but unimportant tasks include things like phone calls that scream to be answered but may not actually be necessary. Your A and B tasks should all be in the top two quadrants, they should all be important, some may be more urgent than others. As you are in transition, you may have a lot of urgent B tasks that need attention but ultimately you should aim to be working in the second quadrant most of the time: doing important but non-urgent A tasks. The more time you spend planning and preparing the work required to achieve your goals, the more that this will be the case.

Now review your As and set them in order of priority among themselves. Assess how long it will take to get each one done and their relative urgency.

Think carefully about the urgency bit: whose agenda makes them urgent?

If it's something that just has to get done by a particular time – like the statute of limitations expiring on a case; showing up for a court appearance; filing something for a deadline; or making sure there's money in the office account to meet the payments – then you better make sure that these things get done by the time they have to. Completing these tasks satisfactorily makes the difference between continuing in practice or not.

But many other urgent things are not really that urgent at all or the urgency flows from someone else's agenda. Test this and see what happens if things don't get done as promptly as they seem to be demanding. You'd be amazed at how some things have a way of resolving themselves, waiting their turn or just not being that pressing after all.

So, now you've got your most important tasks in the right order. Take the top 7; write them down on a piece of paper numbered from 1 to 7 in the order in which they need to be done. You've just got your plan for tomorrow.

Go to your diary for tomorrow onwards and block substantial portions of time in your diary each day. Allocate one, two or three hours each day to start with for time when you will work exclusively on the priorities you have set for yourself. You may need to block longer periods of time eventually when you have better organised how you delegate tasks, etc. but now you are in transition and you will need to deal with all of the other work that you have on hand. Just make sure that you block time for these most important tasks during which time you will work on nothing else and will not allow any distractions.

Treat these blocks of time in your schedule as important appointments that you cannot break. If you had to be in court at a certain time on a certain day there would be no question that you had to be there and that time would be spoken for in your diary. Do the same for the most important things in your business; plan your week in advance, fill the time in your calendar based on what you know you have to do to get through your list of priorities and then stick to that. You've made a commitment to yourself that you must honour.

Of course you'll have to have scope for flexibility here. If the most important thing on your to do list takes longer than you projected you'll have to stick with that until it's done and reschedule accordingly. If genuine emergencies arise they will have to be dealt with. But don't cop out here. Making that commitment to an appointment with yourself is the most important use of your time and you must then hold yourself to it.

When you sit down in that first block of time start on number 1 and do not do anything else until you either finish it or you get to a point where you can't proceed further without input from someone else or something else to be done that you can't do there and then. When, and only when, you get to this point move on to number 2 and so on.

This may seem uncomfortable at first. There may be so many things to do or some of the tasks may seem so large as to be insurmountable. But you have broken the tasks down and thought carefully about their relative order of priority. There is only so much that you can get done in any day and the one thing you now know for certain is that you are working with extreme focus on the most important one.

Next we come back to the Pareto Principle or the 80/20 Rule that I mentioned in Chapter 9. It is so important, that it is worth reviewing again here.

This is the rule that says that 80% of your profits come from 20% of your clients and that 80% of your problems come from another 20% of your clients.

Remember that the rule does not need to follow an exact 80/20 ratio, it can be 90/10 and indeed the numbers don't even need to add up to 100; but the principle is always there: a disproportionately small number of causes result in a large number of effects.

Understanding this principle is one of the most powerful tools in productivity. Focus on the 20% that produces the 80% of the desired outcomes. And it can be leveraged even further: remember too that within that 20% there will be 20% with the same disproportionate level of effect and so on and so forth. Keep this in mind in everything that you do.

Once you do so you will inevitably come to the conclusion that time management in and of itself starts from an incorrect assumption. It is not about getting all that you have to do done each day; it is about identifying what is truly important, prioritising that and then giving yourself time to do it.

> Visualise your life the way you want it: define your vision or your *why*?

- ➤ Set the specific and measurable goals that you need to achieve to realise your vision; give each one a deadline. Write your goals down.
- ➤ Develop action plans to achieve your goals. Break what needs to happen over 3 years down into what you need to get done each year, each month, each week, each day, each hour to keep moving you in the direction of your goals.
- ➤ List everything you have to do and prioritise each item as A, B and C by reference to how doing that thing will help achieve your goals. Put the As in the order of their relative priority.
- ➤ Categorise tasks by their urgency and real importance. You will have to delete or delegate tasks that you can't or shouldn't be doing.
- ➤ Block out time in your calendar in advance; make appointments with yourself to do your most important tasks.
- ➤ Write down the top 7. Start on number 1 tomorrow and don't stop until you have it done or can't progress further without external input. Continue down the order of priorities in this way.

Chapter 20: Managing Distractions

Meetings are an addictive, highly self-indulgent activity that corporations and other organisations habitually engage in only because they cannot actually masturbate.

– Dave Barry

The most powerful tool that you have to achieve your goals is concentrated action. But it has to be focussed and directed and it has to be relentless. So when you are working on what is the most important thing in your business, you must be able to do so without interruption or distraction, otherwise that vital force of concentration will be dissipated.

In the modern office environment, there are three primary sources of distraction and interruption: the phone, email and meetings.

The Phone

Now, before we get into this in detail, let's get something clear: your firm should provide outstanding customer service. That is a given. All of the best marketing in the world will be wasted unless the client's or Prospective Client's experience in dealing with your business is a good one at every stage. So, what I am advocating here is *not* that you treat the clients and Prospective Clients that contact your business with anything other than outstanding customer service in how you handle their calls.

One of the biggest complaints that clients make about lawyers is that they never return their calls. So, you can create a unique selling proposition for yourself just by guaranteeing that you will always do this very simple thing well. For instance you can *promise* that your firm will *always* get back to the caller within a given time period and will ensure that they will always be *guaranteed* to speak to the person they expect to speak to whenever they call in on a *scheduled* call. That's pretty simple, but pretty radical in terms of the experience of many clients in dealing with law firms. And frankly this is the stuff people really care about – not qualifications or years of experience.

However, if you accept calls randomly on a first come first served basis, there's no way you are going to be able to make good on that kind of promise to return calls. That way you are just going to be putting out fires and dealing with continuous interruptions in everything that you do. So, you've got to make some changes if you're going to do this properly and well.

The phone is something that seems to have gotten itself into urgent status by default. When the phone rings, like Pavlov's dogs, we are conditioned to answer it immediately. But why? The only reason the phone is ringing is because someone somewhere dialled a number because they felt like talking to you. But they didn't necessarily check with you first. So why should you be on that call.

Unscheduled phone calls are very often in the third quadrant of Steven Covey's four quadrants we referred to in the last chapter: *seemingly* urgent but not important. You should not be dealing with unscheduled incoming phone calls directly.

In order for this to work you need to make a clear policy. Be honest with people. Have your staff be honest with people. Honesty and integrity should be at the core of your personal and business reputation.

Therefore, don't have people say you're in a meeting if you're not. Develop a coherent policy that your staff fully understand and appreciate so that they can explain why you are not available to take calls. If you were in court arguing a client's case you would not be available to take a call.

So, you and your staff can explain to clients that their work requires your complete undivided attention to get done to the standards that they should expect and that you insist upon. For this reason, any member of staff engaged in important client work won't be available for unscheduled interruptions and that includes phone calls. Your clients shouldn't tolerate having you or your staff interrupted while working on their matter; and you simply afford the same respect and importance to all of your clients' work.

You can also explain to your clients that the work you and your staff do for them is either charged by the hour or priced based on an estimate of how long it is likely to take to get done. Therefore, if you spend time wastefully and inefficiently allowing all interruptions and unscheduled phone calls while working on their matter this is going to involve the work taking a lot longer and consequently costing a lot more. This generally resonates with most reasonable people.

But this does not mean you are unavailable. On the contrary, you work this way in order to ensure that you are *always* available to be on calls that are scheduled in advance. This is how you deliver on your guarantee to your clients always to return their calls.

To really make this effective use a shared calendar in Outlook or on Google Calendar or in a similar package. Block time in advance, setting blocks of clear, inviolable time to carry out the tasks that you have identified as most important based on estimates of how long each task or each part of each task is likely to take. Block time in the calendar each day for returning calls and emails. If that time is available your staff knows that they can schedule a time for you to return the call.

This is where things can get interesting. Develop a written procedure and train your staff to elicit as much information as they can in order to arrange the call. What does the person wish to speak to you about? What are the questions that they wish to ask you? How long is the call likely to take so that it can be scheduled in the diary appropriately? This way your staff can create an agenda for the call. You can have this agenda and the file in advance of the call so that you can prepare for the call comprehensively. Now you will be able to deal with the subject matter of the call really satisfactorily from the client's point of view. You won't be working on the fly, trying to recall details from memory and having to tell clients you'll get back to them after you've checked the file thus necessitating another call. This will also emphasise the importance of the time being expended on the matter for the client by you; time which you can record properly.

Managing Distractions

Perhaps the most important thing in this process is to train your staff in triaging the call in this way to identify if they or someone else in the office may be able to help with or resolve the issue for the client in the first place. They may not need to speak to you at all and may get a much more satisfactory outcome as far as they are concerned in dealing with someone else. This can be a real win–win.

You must follow your own rules and do what you say you'll do here. If you tell someone you're going to get back to them you must call when you promised. *Always*. And when you make time available in your diary to enable staff to schedule calls you have to honour this commitment. You have to be true to the message that you and your staff give out on your behalf. This is all part of the integrity of your personal brand.

Exceptions: you have to have exceptions right? Well to a point of course, but you have to think very carefully about those exceptions and set them very clearly in advance so that everyone is aware of exactly how far they extend and you don't end up having more exceptions than rules.

If you're doing large transactional work or involved in negotiations you will probably need to have an exception for your counterpart on the other side of the transaction or negotiation at key points in the process; e.g. around closings or settlements. Set these clearly with your team and identify by name the person from whom you will accept a call. This could be a standing arrangement for a particular period of time or for that day or that morning. Tailor this to suit. But make sure everyone is on the same page.

Don't get annoyed with someone if they don't put through a call you did want to take, or put through a call that you didn't, if you didn't make it completely clear for them in advance.

Of course if someone is ringing in at a pre-agreed time on a scheduled call make sure that you are available and that the person is put through to you. The person answering the phone should be able to see your calendar and see that this call is scheduled.

You'll also need an exception to deal with short rallies of telephone tennis. You know the scenario: you call the person's mobile, and it rings out while they root around in their handbag or pull over the car. You then try calling them again, their phone is engaged because they're calling you back and then a few minutes later one of you gets a call from the other. In this scenario, make sure that the person taking incoming calls at reception knows you're trying to get through to the other person and puts them through if they're simply ringing back on a call where you were trying to get them.

Next, turn off your mobile phone while you are at your desk.

So far we've been talking about handling phone calls in an office environment where all calls come through a central switch where you can establish a gatekeeper to your time.

But even assuming that you do work a process where a receptionist or secretary screens your calls, all of this comes to nothing if there is a second phone in your room that you will answer whenever it rings. And who hasn't been there when you're stuck on a call in the office and the mobile rings with a call you just have to take and vice versa. The only way in which to prevent this is to turn off your mobile phone when you are at your desk and unavailable to take calls.

Now, if you do have family and other important people in your life who are used to immediate access to you through mobile calls and texts, make sure that they are aware that your phone will be switched off when you are at your desk and that you won't get that text that they are stuck on the side of the road with a flat tyre. Make sure they know that if that happens there is a way to get through to you: perhaps by calling your office and telling the person at the desk that it is genuinely urgent and important.

But remember what I said about emergencies earlier; *let 'em know* that if they cry wolf it better be good – you're at important work and should not be disturbed unless absolutely essential.

While we are on the subject of mobile phones, voicemail on a mobile is a very inefficient means of leaving and taking messages. A message unless written down will almost instantly be forgotten, and because you're using a mobile phone you may well be checking the messages without the facility to write them down. One message in a sequence of many is very often going to be more important or more pressing than the others, and when you get caught up in whatever it takes to react to the message that you need to return first, there is every likelihood that you will overlook or forget others.

Delegate this task and set up a simple process where someone else takes your messages for you which they give to you written down on a list in whatever format works for you. Use voicemail like a central switch, make sure whoever is checking it is writing the messages down and logging them for you. That way nothing gets overlooked or forgotten. For instance you can set the message on your phone to explain to callers that you do not use voicemail on your mobile but that if they ring your office number and leave a message for you there it will *always* receive attention.

Email

One of the great things about email is its immediacy. However, just like the phone, the time that an email is received should not necessarily dictate when you respond to it. Unless it is genuinely urgent.

If you receive an email warning you that someone is going to apply for an injunction later that day in default of some action or your flights are going to be cancelled if you don't confirm your booking by a hard time deadline, you need to pay attention to those ones as they come in.

However, these tend to be rare compared with the tsunami of inane, unnecessary or relatively trivial email sent each day. The addictive part of email is that it is often very easy to deal with it. It is so tempting to ping back a one-liner or a one-worder that deals with the email and gets another job done (albeit perhaps a completely unimportant one).

First, stop checking email all the time. Just being aware that an email has been received is a distraction. If you are at your desk to concentrate on the most important work you have to do and if you become aware in your peripheral vision that an email has appeared in Outlook or if that little reminder in the bottom right hand corner of the screen pops up, your mind is immediately diverted from the important task requiring your complete focus and concentration and is now thinking about the email or the person who sent it.

The client or the matter may be an important one in itself but it can wait, particularly when your clients know how you work. However, your mind is now thinking about it and if it's something that you know you can deal with quickly and easily the temptation to respond is almost irresistible.

But you must resist.

You should set a clear policy that everyone dealing with you understands. Inform all new clients of your communication policy in terms of how this benefits them. You ensure that you give their work the attention it deserves and are always available and on time when you do schedule a time to talk or to meet. In the process you provide them with a clear procedure for phone calls, emails and in-person meetings. Go through this over the phone or face to face when you first meet and are explaining how you work. Include a regular note on how the office works in your newsletter. Make it part of your letter of engagement, provide clear customer service levels in your agreement, make this a significant benefit of dealing with you and make your policy an essential component in your ability to deliver on it.

As for others who don't know you, you need to let them know how you work.

A permanent auto-reply in Outlook is perfect for this. It's the type of thing that is often reserved for when you are out of the office. You can leave it on constantly to provide a very simple message: it will let the person that has sent you an email know how you work. For instance, it can tell them that you do not review emails immediately upon receipt and advise them that if the matter is urgent they should contact the office reception by telephone for further assistance. It could let them know how you review emails and when they can expect a response from you.

So, if a valued client needs urgent assistance, and they're not aware of how you work or have forgotten, they'll get immediate notification letting them know when they can expect to hear from you and providing them with an alternative means of getting in touch if the matter is really urgent. Non-clients needing to get an urgent message to you will also know what to do.

Of course, non-clients won't necessarily appreciate having to work on your terms and unlike your clients won't have agreed to this in advance. But regrettably, this is the price of getting your most important work done.

So, having given your clients and all other third parties who are sending you emails notification of your email policy, you need to work your policy.

First off, if you use Outlook, disable the pop-up notification that email has been received which appears in the bottom right hand corner of your screen. This creates a distraction every time it appears. It is almost impossible to ignore this and not be tempted to have a peek to see the email.

If you use Outlook for managing meeting and call appointments, so that all members of your team know when you are available and when you are not, you may have to have Outlook open during the day to see your calendar. This is tricky, as it is practically impossible not to slip into bad habits and look at the email tab when you should only be looking at the calendar. One solution is to have your Outlook calendar automatically synched with your practice management software or Google Calendar and to use that second calendar which is not linked to your source of email as your main one during the day. That may enable you to share a calendar with everyone you work with without having direct email access. You'll need to tweak this to get something that works for you.

Remember email is like a drug: it is addictive and much easier to fall back into bad habits than not. So this is one area in which you will have to exercise great discipline. But keep in mind the prize: achievement of your most important work and ultimately the progressive realisation of your worthy goals – true success in other words.

After that, batch the time that you do review and respond to emails. For instance, you could chose 30-minute periods twice a day at say 12.30pm and 4pm. The first time is just before lunch and allows you to deal with any relatively urgent emails from the first half of the day. Done this way, all emails of the day can be dealt with in much less than an hour in total, rather than being a constant distraction throughout the day. This time can be combined with your time for returning phone calls, making it a really intensive period of catch up and doubly productive as a result.

Consider having someone else triage your emails first. Give them discretion, let them know your ground rules and what you want to achieve. Let them know the emails they have complete discretion with and the ones that you wish to be left for you. This can eliminate a huge number of the relatively trivial work-related emails that clog up the majority of the inbox. You can be certain that the 80/20 principle is hard at work here as much as in every other area of your business and you should harness it.

Structure your email responses so that they do not require a reply if a reply is not necessary. Multiple emails saying, "Thanks" or "You're welcome" can add to the clutter. You need to be firm and professional but not come across as rude or discourteous; you just need to make it clear in your email that it does not warrant a response if you are not seeking one.

Finally, if you go to all of this trouble to put up effective barriers to the email time vampires at your desk, do not let them come around the defences via your pocket. As with phone calls, when you are at your desk turn off your smart phone so that you are not tempted to have a sneaky peek at emails on it, just to satisfy your cravings for a fix. Don't worry; after a little while you'll be completely detoxified.

Meetings

After you've dealt with the phone and email, the next biggest potential source of interruption and distraction is the face-to-face meeting. These take many forms and you need techniques for dealing with each.

First off is the impromptu meeting or drop-in. There are two main categories: those from outside and those from within. Then there are scheduled meetings.

1.   Unscheduled Callers from Outside the Office:

Personal callers from outside pose many of the same considerations as those ringing into the office on the phone. The key point that you want to emphasise politely but firmly is that you guarantee that you will always be available and on time to meet anyone coming to a *scheduled* appointment. Your office isn't like those bastions of inefficiency where clients are left sitting in the waiting room because you've organised your day badly and are running behind because you've gotten stuck on another call and someone popped in 10 minutes before who kept you back. That is the experience of many clients in many professional offices. Make yours a refreshing change in its friendly efficiency. When people call to reception the first thing that they should be asked by your smiling receptionist after having been warmly greeted by name is whether they have an appointment. This simple question alone makes its own point. The next thing the person at reception should do is to find out whether something urgent has come up that needs immediate attention or whether it's something that can be resolved without an appointment. If not the next available mutually convenient appointment time can be set there and then.

There is one fundamentally important impromptu caller that you have to provide for here, both in a phone and in-person call context. That is a new enquiry from a Prospective Client who has not dealt with your business before. This person will not be aware of how you operate and may be an important source of new business. Here you need to have a procedure in place to make sure that this person's interaction with your business works for them from the outset. When everyone in your business is working to pre-scheduled calls and appointments in between blocks of time set for particular tasks, an unscheduled caller is going to interrupt *someone*; this is unavoidable. In this situation you need to have an agreed procedure to treat the new enquiry like a caller to a hotline, whoever is available will take the call and make sure that the caller gets a satisfactory response. If the person who has to field the call isn't able to deal with the caller's query there and then, they will always be able to reassure the caller that they've come to the right place and that the person with whom they need to speak will get back to them within an agreed time frame. The follow-up on that call then becomes an urgent priority that must be scheduled immediately.

2. Unscheduled Callers from Inside:

The second type of drop-in caller is from within your own organisation. The most dangerous five words to your productivity are: "Have you got a minute?" The answer to which should generally be *no*.

There are exceptions to this: if the building is on fire, please let people know that they should feel free to open your door, interrupt you and tell you to evacuate the building. They should feel completely justified in interrupting you in other comparable situations of this nature. Apart from that, they should not.

If a person comes to you with a non-urgent request for some of your time, don't refuse them but give them a scheduled time slot in the near future to which you will commit to sitting down with them and resolving all of their issues. Ask them to set those issues out for you in writing in the meantime so that you have a clear agenda of what needs to be worked through. This will be doubly productive. It will make the other person think through their issues clearly and given time they may be able to resolve them on their own. When they come to meet you, you will both have a far more productive and satisfactory meeting working through a very clear agenda of items requiring attention. You may often find that the other person is reluctant to commit to that meeting at all thus calling into question the reason for the interruption in the first place.

Remember that this is a two-way street. You can only expect others to respect your time to the extent that you respect and value theirs. So take the same approach with others as you expect them to take with you.

3. Scheduled Meetings:

After you've eliminated unscheduled interruptions, the next type of in-person meetings that you have to address are scheduled ones. Sometimes this is unavoidable, necessary and productive; but often it is none of these.

The first thing to establish is whether the meeting is necessary at all. Often when clients contact you requesting a meeting a little effective communication can establish that a face-to-face meeting is not required. No-one likes having to take time out of their busy schedule to travel to your office to meet in-person to deal with something that could have been dealt with without that hassle. Again, this is not about being inaccessible, it's the complete opposite: it is about achieving the most mutually satisfactory outcome at every stage of the Client Fulfilment process. It should be an enhanced level of service that you are completely focussed on delivering all of the time.

If it's an internal office meeting (and I'm a big fan of regular, effective internal office meetings) consider carefully who needs to be there. Don't have people present when they don't need to be, this is the worst waste of everyone's time. Then make sure the meetings have a clear agenda and give each agenda item a time frame to which you stick religiously. Then make sure the meeting is chaired properly and that the agenda is adhered to. Don't let people wander off topic. The meeting should be minuted with clear actions arising from each agenda item; each action item needs to be assigned to a named individual at the meeting, with a date set for when it will be done and recorded in the minutes. Minimise the follow-up work required in writing up minutes by having them recorded there and then at the meeting on a laptop or tablet; use an app such as Evernote which is an excellent tool for collaboration and tracking progress on actions. The agenda, minutes and follow-up items can be shared, assigned, accessed and updated constantly by all in attendance on their desktops, laptops, tablets and smartphones.

Take Time Out

If you put these procedures in place, you will have increased your productivity significantly and you will encounter minimal interruption in the focussed pursuit of the most important tasks required to achieve your goals. But you will still not be completely interruption free. With the best systems and will in the world that will always remain impossible while you are in the office. But there is a solution: find a cave.

You need a cave where you can go away from the office to work completely alone. It needs to be a place without a phone or WIFI and preferably not known about by anyone but you. You need to schedule time in your calendar to go there regularly and take time out to work on the most important task of all: thinking and reviewing your goals, the vision behind them, the action plans required to take you towards them, their respective priorities and the systems you need to implement to achieve it all. You can close the door in the office and unplug the phone, but you just know there'll always be something that will justify that quick interruption when everyone knows you're there.

OK, it need not be an actual cave. It could be a public library (but if you choose this option make sure it's somewhere you're not likely to meet anyone you know), a cheap rented back office, or a box room somewhere. Just make it somewhere where you can go to be alone and undisturbed for an extended period at least once a week to think and to plan and to review your goals and your progress towards them with complete focus.

Phone

- Control and minimise unscheduled phone calls.
- Create a policy and be honest with people. But be clear and firm.
- Make sure your staff understand the policy and have a clear procedure to follow. Don't place them in compromising situations.
- Use a shared calendar with your staff. Block time and allow time for returning calls and emails so that your staff can tell people when you will return their calls.
- Work with your staff so that they can deal with more and more of the calls without your involvement.
- Have exceptions for urgent or important matters but don't have more exceptions than rules.
- Turn off your mobile phone at your desk.
- Don't use voicemail; delegate your message handling.

Email

- ➢ Stop checking email; it is a constant distraction. Turn off the notifications that you have received email. Resist the temptation to reply quickly just because you can. Only check email twice a day.
- ➢ Set a policy as with the phone. Set an automatic reply to notify others of your policy.
- ➢ Block time during the day to reply to email in batches. Have someone else triage your inbox.
- ➢ Do not look at email on your smart phone just because you've disabled it on your desktop; turn off your mobile phone.

Meetings

- ➢ Cut out unnecessary meetings. Stop drop-ins – both internal and external. Have a clear policy.
- ➢ Have appropriate exceptions and procedures for new enquiries from people who don't know the policy.
- ➢ For non-urgent unscheduled requests of your time from people working with you, give the person a scheduled time slot and ask them to set out the purpose of the meeting in writing in advance.
- ➢ Consider every meeting in terms of whether it is necessary and whether all of the parties due to attend need to be there.
- ➢ Have a written agenda, chair meetings properly, keep minutes and have action items with deadlines and

clearly assigned personal responsibility for each. Use an app like Evernote for collaboration and follow up.

Time Out

> ➤ Have a cave: somewhere outside of the office where you can go to take scheduled time out regularly and to work without any distractions whatsoever.

Chapter 21: Next Steps

Your present circumstances don't determine where you can go; they merely determine where you start.

– Nido Qubein

You've covered a lot of ground in a short space of time, much of which may seem unfamiliar and uncomfortable. Don't be tempted to just put this book down and say, "Na, not for me, that'll never work in my practice".

It will work and it is for you.

The only thing I know for sure is that this stuff works. I'm a practising solicitor just like you and everything that I have shared with you in this book has been based on my own experience in a real life Real Law firm. It is all supported by objective, reproducible and independently verifiable evidence of it working in everyday practice in an Irish solicitors' office.

And it is reproducible by you in your Real Law firm. You will need to refine and adapt it for your niche and your target market (once you've defined it) but the only important thing to be clear on is that you certainly can.

No, it is not a magic formula for success. What you have here are just the ideas and the tools. They are very valuable ideas and tools, but without implementation and hard work they are useless.

However, if you adopt the ideas and use the tools, and actually do the work of implementing them in your business, you will succeed. You will develop the successful legal business that you need to enable you to live the life you want no matter what the economic conditions, the competitive environment or the regulatory regime.

It may seem daunting, like there's just too much to do, that it's too complicated or that you don't have the skills. Well, there is a lot to do, but it's modular. You don't have to do it all at once in a big bang (you can if you wish, but you don't have to). You can start wherever you think will be most beneficial for you and what you want to achieve for your Real Law firm and then keep adding to it.

The important thing is that you do start. And then persevere.

You may wonder, "Hang on, part of what this book is all about is focussing on my specialist area of expertise, how on Earth am I expected to be able to do that and be a jack-of-all-trades in the marketing department?"

Well, of course, you don't have to do it all yourself. You may be quite sure that you're never going to write and design ad copy or put together the mechanics of an AdWords campaign. You don't necessarily have to; you can buy in these skills or outsource them. But now, when you do so, you'll know what you're looking for. You'll have a strategy and a clear idea of what you want to achieve. You'll know how to select the right message for your market and the media that might work best for that. You'll understand direct response principles, know the objective of your marketing and how to measure and test its effectiveness.

The only two things that you can't get out of doing are deciding what you want and then doing the work required to get it.

So, if you're wondering where to start, that's my strongest recommendation, get crystal clear on what you want from all of this and why you are doing it in the first place. Then take action; preferably massive action.

In order to get you started, I have put together a quick-start how-to pack to get you moving fast. It will take you through a simple step-by-step process to develop an immediate action plan for your Real Law firm.

Start now and just go to:

www.TheSolicitorsGuide.com/resources

One Other Thing

Finally, you'll appreciate that this book has been written at a time when we stand on the brink of very significant change in the legal profession in the form of the Legal Services Regulation Bill. I had considered holding off on publishing this book until after the Bill was enacted but while we have been promised the new legislation for a very long time who knows when we finally will have it.

So this is to some extent a preliminary edition of the book that I intend updating as soon as the new Act is passed and the outline of the new regulatory regime is clearer. As soon as this is the case, I will be preparing a supplementary update to this edition and I will send you a copy with my compliments.

Please go to the link below now and get on the priority notification list to receive your copy of the Legal Services Regulation Act update as soon as it is available:

www.TheSolicitorsGuide.com/resources

Further Reading

The man who does not read good books has no advantage over the man who can't read them.

— Mark Twain

L earning what I have shared with you in this book has involved a lot of reading. If you are interested in reading further in this area (and I recommend that you do) I have distilled this down for you into a reading list grouping the most important books by the areas to which they relate with a short commentary on each.

To get immediate access to your free copy of this list go to:

www.TheSolicitorsGuide.com/resources

About the Author

I'm a practising solicitor just like you who has been working in the trenches of Real Law for twenty years, mostly at close quarters in hand-to-hand fighting.

In recent years I have become consumed with marketing and business development for solicitors and this book draws together my study and experience in that area for your benefit.

While the only important measure of any of this are the results it has produced under the bonnet in a real life Real Law firm, there have been some more externally visible successes too. One of these came when our firm's website which was designed entirely along the principles outlined for you here won Legal Website of the Year at the Irish Law Awards 2014. Another was when I was shortlisted as one of four Marketers of the Year at Ben Glass's Great Legal Marketing Summit 2014 in Arlington, Virginia, where I was asked to present the results of our success to over 350 lawyers from all across the USA, Canada and the rest of the world.

The reason I wrote this book is that I passionately believe in a better and brighter future for Irish Real Lawyers in private practice.

That is why I have shared the benefit of my research and experience with you.

If you'd like to learn more, go to:

www.TheSolicitorsGuide.com/resources

Glossary

Ad group: A group of display ads on Google AdWords or Bing Ads.

AIDA formula: The system of writing to attract Attention, create Interest, cultivate Desire and prompt Action.

Autoresponder: A computer program that sends email automatically to individuals or lists of individuals often as part of a pre-determined sequence.

Banner ads: (or web banners) Ads placed on the websites of third parties intended to attract traffic to the website of the advertiser by a link from the banner ad.

B2B: Business to business

B2C: Business to consumer

Black hat: SEO and social media methods that are not authorised by the search engines or social media sites or are in breach of the terms of use, the practice of which can lead to the practitioner's website being blacklisted or social media account suspended etc.

Blog: (an abbreviation of the expression weblog) A discussion or informational site published on the Web and consisting of discrete entries ("posts") typically displayed in reverse chronological order (the most recent post appearing first).

Brand advertising: Advertising primarily intended to promote the brand and identity of the advertiser by reference to things such as its name, symbol, slogan or features.

Call to action: An instruction to the reader, listener or viewer to provoke an immediate response, usually using an imperative verb such as "call now", "find out more" or "click here".

Campaign: A series of ads that share a single idea and theme. In Google AdWords, a Campaign is made up of a series of ad groups in turn made up of a series of ads.

Client Fulfilment: The legal work you do for a client after they have agreed to become a client.

Client Profiles: Personas that you should create in as much detail as possible to describe your Ideal Client and your Client from Hell in each of your practice areas.

Control: The control is the best performing version of an ad against which changes to the ad copy are tested one change at a time. Tests performing better than the old control then become the new control.

Cookies: Also known as HTTP cookies, web cookies, Internet cookies or browser cookies, are small pieces of data sent from a website and stored in a visitor's web browser while the visitor is browsing that website. Every time the visitor loads the website, the browser sends the cookie back to the server to notify the website of the visitor's previous activity.

Copy: The text or content of an ad or marketing piece.

Copywriter: Someone who writes copy.

Contact Relationship Management (CRM): A system for managing a firm's interactions with current and Prospective Clients. CRM software uses technology to organise, automate and synchronise the process.

Glossary

Demographics: An analysis of your target market by structure of population; factors such as age, location, family status, occupation, income, etc.

Display network: The network of websites, videos and apps where your pay-per-click ads can appear without the necessity for anyone to have searched for them based on keywords.

Direct mail: Physical correspondence sent via the postal service.

Direct Response: The system of marketing and advertising the primary purpose of which is to provoke a direct response in the reader, listener or viewer through the use of a call to action.

Follow up: The system of communication with a Lead after he or she has expressed some interest in your Real Law Firm or some element of its marketing.

Friends: Other Facebook users who have connected with you on Facebook.

Funnel: A marketing or business development system consisting of Lead Generation processes at the wide mouth of the funnel and Lead Conversion processes at the narrow neck of the funnel feeding into a Client Fulfilment pipeline.

Grok: Understand something intuitively or by empathy.

Headline: The title line that should be given additional prominence at the top of every ad or marketing piece the sole purpose of which is to attract attention to the piece and progress the reader to the next line.

Key Performance Indicators (KPIs): Performance measurements that evaluate the success of a Real Law Firm or of a particular activity in which it engages.

Keywords: The words entered by the user of a search engine to describe what it is that they are looking for.

Lag indicators: Measurements of the effect produced by causes; the results that lag behind the activity that produces them.

Landing page: A page on a website on which traffic from a specific source lands. Analysis of traffic to a landing page can help determine the effectiveness of the source in generating traffic and the quality of that traffic.

Lead: A Prospective Client who has expressed an interest in a service that your Real Law firm provides.

Lead Conversion: The process of a converting a Lead into a client in your Real Law firm.

Lead indicators: Measurements of the causes that produce effects; the leading activity that produces the results that lag behind.

Lead Generation: The process of generating new Leads for your Real Law firm.

Like: To click an icon on a post on Facebook (usually shown as a "thumbs-up" icon) signifying approval of or agreement with the post.

List: Your list of all current and past clients of your Real Law firm along with all Prospective Clients who have identified themselves as Leads.

Mindset: Your established set of assumptions and attitudes that creates a powerful incentive within you to adopt or accept certain behaviours, choices or tools.

Most desired action: On any page of your website the most desired action is what you wish the visitor to do on that page. The call to action on that page should be focussed on your most desired action.

National Directory Database (NDD): A list of all phone numbers printed in public directories or available through directory enquiries. The NDD contains an opt-out register on which phone line subscribers may record their preference not to receive direct marketing calls. Requests to opt out are made via the phone line provider.

News feed: On a Facebook page, the news feed is the constantly updating list of stories in the middle of your home page. The news feed includes status updates, photos, videos, links, app activity and likes from people, Pages and groups that you follow on Facebook.

News jacking: A public relations technique involving piggybacking on the attention of the news media on another item.

Parade of interest: The continually moving and varying state of interest of a Prospective Client's mind in any given subject or service. The effectiveness of any marketing piece will depend on the extent to which its contents coincide with the Prospective Client's level of interest at the point in time at which it appears.

Pay-per-click (PPC): Advertising on the Internet which you pay for each time (but only when) a Prospective Client clicks on it.

Pipeline: A Client Fulfilment pipeline is the system of work flow that starts when a client with a new matter enters your Real Law Firm and ends when that matter is completed producing fees and a satisfied client.

Podcasting: The creation and broadcast on the web of digital audio recordings (called podcasts) which are subscribed to and downloaded through web syndication or streamed on-line to computers and mobile devices.

Positioning: Creating a position in the mind of those in your target market that identifies what you do in terms of a problem that they are experiencing, the unique benefits that you provide in being able to solve it and why they should chose you ahead of every alternative available in the market in order to do so.

Prospective Client: Someone with the potential to be a client but who may not have yet expressed any interest in your Real Law firm.

Psychographics: An analysis of your target market by how they think and act; factors such as personality, values, opinions, attitudes, interests, lifestyles etc.

Public Relations (PR): The practice of managing the spread of information between your firm and the public generally via the media.

Organic traffic: Also referred to as organic search is unpaid traffic to your website that has found your website based solely on its relevance to the keywords submitted to the search engine.

Real Law: The 92% of the Irish legal profession comprising small and medium law firms consisting of 5 partners or less.

Real Lawyer: A lawyer practising in Real Law who doesn't just want to own a job, but rather wants to be entrepreneurial and create a successful business.

Remarketing: Also known as retargeting is the system of showing pay-per-click ads to a browser of the web based on their previous search history.

Return on Investment (ROI): For any marketing piece the ratio of what is spent on that piece to the fees that are produced as a direct result of that piece is the return on investment of that piece.

Search engine: A software system that is designed to search for information on the web by running an algorithm on a web crawler.

Search Engine Optimisation (SEO): That practice or set of practices that web developers engage in to ensure that their websites are optimised for search engines.

Search Engine Results Page (SERP): The page served up by a search engine with a list of results in response to a search query with results listed from most relevant to least relevant based on the keywords chosen for the search.

Search network: The network of Search Engine Results Pages (SERPs) where pay-per-click ads can be shown alongside organic search results based on their relevance to the keywords on which those searches were based.

Segmentation: Involves dividing the broad target market for legal services into subsets of Prospective Clients, who have common needs and priorities, and then designing and implementing strategies to target them.

Selling off the page: Seeking to sell a product or service directly from a page on a website.

Shock and awe pack: An information package to be sent to a Prospective Client or new client designed to have maximum impact by virtue of the quality, variety and extent of its contents.

Sidebar: On a social media site such as Facebook or LinkedIn a visual area to the side of the main News Feed display where pay-per-click ads can be shown.

Spam: Originally referred to junk email or unsolicited bulk email involving nearly identical messages sent to numerous recipients by email but now extends to refer to all kinds of similarly abusive uses of electronic and online media.

Traffic: Web traffic is the amount of data sent and received by visitors to a web site. In this book traffic is used to refer to all Prospective Clients sent to your marketing funnel from all online and offline sources.

Uniform Resource Locator (URL): In the context of the web is a reference to a web page that specifies the location of the page on the web and a mechanism for retrieving it; e.g. a web address such as: www.thisisaurl.com

Unique Selling Proposition (USP): Why anyone in the market would chose you above every other alternative available in the marketplace.

White hat: Legitimate SEO and social media methods which are authorised by the search engines or social media sites and compliant with their terms of use.

Appendix 1: Solicitors' Professional Regulations

Now, before we get into this, let's be clear: this is my take on the Regulations, but you're a solicitor, so you form your own view. This is not a legal text book and my review doesn't purport to be any definitive statement of the law or the operation of the regulatory regime. If that's what you're looking for, read the Acts, read the Regulations and talk to the regulator directly before you do anything.

The Solicitors (Amendment) Act, 2002 allowed solicitors to advertise. The provisions of the Act were implemented in the Solicitors Advertising Regulations 2002.

For me, the most important Regulation, and the one that we should take as our starting point is Regulation 3, which reads as follows:

"Subject to these Regulations, it shall be lawful for a solicitor to advertise."

At the time of writing the Legal Services Regulation Bill is at an advanced stage in the Dáil and the indications are that its enactment will be given priority. We have been told this since the bill was first published in 2011, so we shall see. But we expect to be looking at a completely new regulatory regime sooner or later.

In the meantime, we remain governed by the 2002 Regulations made pursuant to the 2002 Act, which in turn amended Section 71 of the Solicitors Act, 1954. And one would imagine that even if the Legal Services Regulation Bill is enacted in the short term, we will continue to be governed by the existing Regulations for some time while the Authority is established and everything that will be required to go along with that put in place.

For the purposes of this review I will stick to the Regulations. This is where the rubber tends to hit the road from a practical perspective in deciding how you as a practitioner might advertise your practice.

Regulation 2 defines advertising as follows:

"*advertisement* means any communication (whether oral or in written or other visual form and whether produced by electronic or other means) which is intended to publicise or otherwise promote a solicitor in relation to the solicitor's practice, including –

(i)   any brochure, notice, circular, leaflet, poster, placard, photograph, illustration, emblem, display, stationery, directory entry, article or statement for general publication,

(ii)   any electronic address or any information provided by the solicitor that is accessible electronically,

(iii)   any audio or video recording, or

(iv)   any presentation, lecture, seminar or interview

which is so intended but excluding a communication which is primarily intended to give information on the law."

So the definition of advertising is pretty comprehensive. I'll deal first of all with what the Regulations state that you specifically can't do and then get to my take on what that leaves you with.

Regulation 4(a) states that

Solicitor's Professional Regulations

"An advertisement intended to publicise or otherwise promote a solicitor in relation to the solicitor's practice shall be in such a form as shall not –

(i)   be likely to bring the solicitors' profession into disrepute;

(ii)   be in bad taste;

(iii)   reflect unfavourably on other solicitors;

(iv)   contain an express or implied assertion by a solicitor that he has specialist knowledge in any area of law or practice superior to other solicitors (except to the extent that may be permitted under any regulations made pursuant to section 71(8) (as inserted by section 4 of the Act of 2002) of the Act of 1954);

(v)   be false or misleading in any respect;

(vi)   be published in an inappropriate location;

(vii) be in conflict with clause (b) of this Regulation or any other provision of these Regulations;

(viii) expressly or impliedly refer to –

    (I)   claims or possible claims for damages for personal injuries,

    (II)   the possible outcome of claims for damages for personal injuries, or

    (III) the provision of legal services by the solicitor in connection with such claims;

(ix)   expressly or impliedly solicit, encourage or offer any inducement to any person or group or class of persons to make the claims mentioned in sub-clause (viii) of this clause or to contact the solicitor concerned with a view to such claims being made; or

(x)   be contrary to public policy."

Most of these restrictions include the types of things that you might expect such as things bringing the profession into disrepute, that are in bad taste or that are false or misleading. However, Regulation 4(a)(iv) referring to specialist knowledge and 4(a)(viii) referring to personal injury claims appear unduly restrictive at first glance, but I'll come back to these in a moment.

Regulation 4(b) goes on to state that:

"An advertisement published or caused to be published by a solicitor shall not include more than –

(i)   the name, address (including any electronic address), telephone number, facsimile number, place or places of business of the solicitor and any reference to the location of information provided by the solicitor that is accessible electronically;

(ii)   particulars of the academic and professional qualifications and legal experience of the solicitor;

(iii)   (subject to clause (a) of this Regulation) factual information on the legal services provided by the solicitor and on any areas of law to which those services relate;

(iv)   (subject to any regulations made pursuant to section 71(6) (as inserted by section 4 of the Act of 2002) of the Act of 1954) particulars of any charge or fee payable to the solicitor for the provision of any specified legal service; and

(v)   the other information (relating to the solicitor's practice) specified in Regulation 5(a)."

Again, when you look at this at first, you might be tempted to just close the book and go back to hoping that prospective customers will just wander in the door through random chance. The most salient thing that you are allowed to include is your name and address; whoopee! And your academic qualifications; exactly what I've been telling you they're not interested in. But stick with me, the key's in 4(b)(iii) and I'll come back to that after I finish the boring bits.

The "other information (relating to the solicitor's practice) specified in Regulation 5(a)" relates primarily to practical matters like hours of business, announcements of changes to staff and premises. It also includes making references to clients and transactions in ads and includes provision that they may only be made with the client's consent; which you would be obliged to do anyway arising out of your obligation of confidentiality, common sense and courtesy (combined with your basic instinct for self-preservation in not wanting to permanently alienate the client by mentioning them in an ad without their permission – but I digress).

Regulation 6 is quite positive, it says where advertisements may be published and it includes most means. However, it does not include specific reference to the Internet. This is perhaps understandable given the age of the Regulations, but the definition of advertising goes further than Regulation 6 and makes specific reference to "any electronic address or any information provided by the solicitor that is accessible electronically" and Regulation 10 is also quite specifically concerned with the Internet in a restrictive provision. So, while Regulation 6 does not refer to the Internet specifically as a place where advertisements may be published it does include publication by "general circulation whether by post, by hand or electronically" and in practice it seems to be generally accepted as permissible.

Interestingly, the first medium permitted by Regulation 6 is "on television" and despite this open invitation I'm not aware that any Irish lawyers have taken to the small screen in any significant way in the years since the Regulations were introduced. We do seem to be inundated with ads from English law firms and claims agencies on daytime TV, but that's another day's work.

Regulation 7 provides that advertisements shall not be published in inappropriate locations, on any form of transport, in a newspaper on the same page as death notices or on radio immediately before or after death notices. With the exception of the rather odd prohibition on ads on transport, this all seems pretty sensible.

Regulations 8 and 9 get into the specifics of personal injuries advertising.

Regulation 8 contains the provision that an advertisement which contains a reference to "personal injuries" or other contentious business shall include a clear reference to the prohibition contained in S.68(2) of the Solicitors Act, 1954 preventing a solicitor from acting for a client in connection with any contentious business (other than debt collection) on the basis that all or any part of the charges to the client are to be calculated as a specified percentage or proportion of the damages or other moneys that may be payable to the client.

Regulation 8 goes on to provide that wherever the words "personal injuries" appear an asterisk (*) should be placed after the words "personal injuries" that would notate the presence of the following words that should be shown adjacent thereto: "*In contentious business, a solicitor may not calculate fees or other charges as a percentage or proportion of any award or settlement."

Regulation 8 then goes on to clarify that these provisions relating to the words "personal injuries" in any advertisement extend to any other word or words that may be more specifically descriptive of categories of cases where claims for damages for personal injuries may arise, such as "motor accidents", "workplace accidents", "public place accidents" and other words or phrases of a similar nature.

Regulation 9 contains more specific restriction on personal injuries advertising and provides that an advertisement published by a solicitor shall not include the words:

- No win no fee
- No foal no fee
- Free first consultation
- Most cases settle out of court
- Insurance cover arranged to cover legal costs

or other words and phrases of a similar nature which could be construed as meaning that legal services involving contentious business would be provided by the solicitor at no cost or reduced cost to the client.

Regulation 9 goes on to state that an advertisement published by a solicitor shall not include any cartoons, dramatic or emotive words or pictures or make reference to a calamitous event or situation or refer to a willingness to make hospital or home visits. Regulation 9 also states that an ad on a poster or placard (which includes billboard or hoarding) shall not include more than the name, address and basic contact details of the solicitor.

Regulation 10 specifically contemplates the Internet and states that where an ad that is accessible electronically links to other information that is accessible electronically elsewhere, the solicitor shall be personally responsible for the publication of that other information.

Regulation 11 deals with very specific provisions on the size and placing of advertisements which in general terms states that ads must be proportionate to the medium in which they are placed and where factual information on different categories of services is provided, no particular area can be given disproportionate prominence in size or position over any other area. Regulation 11 also states that where an ad is placed close to a solicitor's ad that can reasonably be constructed as relating to or elaborating on the solicitor's ad, the solicitor shall be responsible for that ad.

Regulation 11 also contains a provision in relation to associations: where a solicitor publishes an ad that includes reference to his or her membership of an association made up wholly or mainly of solicitors, that solicitor shall be deemed to be responsible for any advertisement published by that association.

Finally for this section of the review, Regulation 13 provides that a direct unsolicited approach may not be made to any person who is not an existing client with a view to being instructed to provide legal services, where this is likely to bring the solicitors' profession into disrepute.

So far I have been doing exactly what I have been giving out about at the start of the book and telling you everything you can't do. There's a reason for that. You need to be fully conversant with and compliant with the Regulations. *Like 'em or lump 'em, them's the rules* and you've got to abide by them.

If you want to change the rules; get out there and lobby your public representative. Don't take this attitude that because a particular rule is a bad rule it shouldn't apply to you and you can ignore it; your professional integrity and reputation are on the line here.

Some practitioners have just decided to flout the Regulations; the most cursory search of the Internet can demonstrate this. But even if you were willing to consider this, leaving aside the regulatory and reputational issues that would be associated with such a course of action, commercially it would be insane. If you were to build your business model on non-compliant advertising you have to accept that one day, someone is going to call you up or knock on the door and tell you to stop (quite apart from the regulatory and reputational unpleasantness that could follow after that). That means your business model is terminated with extreme prejudice – never a good look.

So, legally, morally, ethically, professionally and commercially, it just makes sense to ensure that, whatever you do, you do it in full compliance with Regulations. That's why I've gone through the detail of the Regulations here in as stimulating a fashion as I could manage without actually asking you to watch paint dry.

But wait, there's hope.

Remember Regulation 3:

"Subject to these Regulations, it shall be lawful for a solicitor to advertise."

And remember Regulation 4(b)(iii) being one of the things that an ad shall not include more than:

"factual information on the legal services provided by the solicitor and on any areas of law to which those services relate"

And remember what I told you earlier: *it's not about you*; they're not interested in where you went to school, your qualifications, your years of combined experience, the quality and good taste of your reception furniture.

Are you noticing a pattern here?

I'm going to give you a hint: factual information about the law and the legal services that you provide in terms of how it can benefit the people who need your help. The Solicitors Advertising Regulations 2002 are practically a manual for content marketing for solicitors. They even tell you how to do it.

But wait, there's more:

Regulation 12; did I mention Regulation 12? It provides a world of opportunity for the astute content marketer. Here's how it goes:

"(a)   The following shall be deemed not to be an advertisement but to be a communication which is primarily intended to give information on the law:

(i)   subject to clause (b) of this Regulation, a book on a legal topic written by a solicitor,

(ii)   subject to clause (c) of this Regulation, an article on a legal topic written by a solicitor where no part of the space of which is paid for by or on behalf of the solicitor;

(iii)   or subject to clause (c) of this Regulation, an oral presentation or media interview given by a solicitor relating to a legal topic where no part of it is paid for by or on behalf of the solicitor.

(b)   In relation to subclause (i) of clause (a) of this Regulation, the circulation by a solicitor to persons (whether or not on request) at no cost or reduced cost to such persons of a book on a legal topic written by the solicitor may be deemed not to be a communication which is primarily intended to give information on the law but rather to be in fact a communication which is primarily intended to publicise or otherwise promote the solicitor in relation to the solicitor's practice.

(c)   In relation to subclauses (ii) and (iii) of clause (a) of this Regulation, a repeated publication of the same or substantially similar article on a legal topic written by a solicitor or the repeated oral presentation or media interview given by a solicitor on the same or substantially similar legal topic may be deemed not to be a communication which is primarily intended to give information on the law but rather to be in fact a communication which is primarily intended to publicise or otherwise promote the solicitor in relation to the solicitor's practice."

Furthermore, Regulation 4(d) states that:

"For the avoidance of doubt, a reference in an advertisement published or caused to be published by a solicitor to his or her authorship of a publication on a legal topic shall be deemed to be factual information on the legal services provided by the solicitor and on any areas of law to which those services relate (as provided for in sub-clause (iii) of clause (b) of this Regulation)."

And this just makes sense; solicitors have to be able to provide clients and Prospective Clients with factual information about the law and the legal services that they provide and the Regulations clearly provide for this.

But let's go back to Regulation 4(a)(iv) which provided that an ad shall be in such a form as shall not:

"contain an express or implied assertion by a solicitor that he has specialist knowledge in any area of law or practice superior to other solicitors (except to the extent that may be permitted under any regulations made pursuant to section 71(8) (as inserted by section 4 of the Act of 2002) of the Act of 1954);"

How do you reconcile this with my suggestion that you specialise and position yourself within your market as such a specialist?

Again content is the key. But before I get into that, let's look at the wording of the Regulation a little more closely.

First of all we have the prohibition against making any express or implied assertion that you have specialist knowledge superior to other solicitors. That is not to say that you cannot choose to specialise in a particular area and state that fact; you simply can't say or imply that you have superior knowledge as a result. And I do not suggest that you do.

What I do suggest you do is create valuable content for your market based on factual information about the law and the legal services you provide that will demonstrate your knowledge and the specialism you have chosen to your target market. Make sure it is relevant, interesting and helpful to your target market.

And then let your information speak for you.

Like I said: *it's not about you.*

OK, so that's the current regime. What are we likely to be faced with in the future? Let's take a look.

At present, the provisions relating to advertising of legal services are contained in Section 151 of the Legal Services Regulation Bill , 2011.

Section 151(1) provides that the Legal Services Regulation Authority may, with the consent of the Minister, make regulations in relation to the advertising of legal services.

Section 151(2) goes on to state what those regulations may specifically provide and includes provision that an advertisement published by a legal practitioner shall be confined to specific information, including-

"(i)　　　　the name, address (including any electronic address), website address, telephone number, facsimile number, place or places of business of the legal practitioner,

(ii)　　　　particulars of the academic and professional qualifications and legal experience of the legal practitioner,

(iii)　　　　factual information on the legal services provided by the legal practitioner and on any areas of law to which those services relate, and

(iv)   particulars of any charge or fee payable to the legal practitioner for the provision of any specified legal service."

These are broadly similar to the provisions of Section 71(3) of the Solicitors Act, 1954 as inserted by the Solicitors Amendment Act, 2002 on which the 2002 Regulations were based, and you will of course note the similarity to Regulation 4(b).

However, there is a fifth category in Section 71(3) of the 1954 Act which allowed for "any other information specified in regulations". The 2002 Regulations did allow for additional information in Regulation 4(b)(v) which is more specifically listed in Regulation 5(a) and you may recall includes things like changes to staff, premises, membership of associations and details of clients and transactions (with the client's consent).

It seems odd that Section 151 (2)(c) of the Bill does not specifically refer to additional information to be provided for by regulation.

Section 151(3) specifies that a legal practitioner shall not publish or cause to be published an advertisement which:

"(a)   is likely to bring the profession of legal practitioner into disrepute,

(b)   is in bad taste,

(c)   reflects unfavourably on other legal practitioners,

(d)   is false or misleading in any respect,

(e)   is published in an inappropriate location, or

(f)   does not comply with regulations under *subsection (1)*."

This section is very similar to Section 71(2) of the 1954 Act, pursuant to which Regulation 4(a) of the 2002 Regulations were made, with a number of very notable exceptions however.

First of all, Section 71(2)(d) contained a prohibition on a reference to specialist knowledge. This is absent from the Bill as currently drafted, this is welcome and in line with the recommendations of the Competition Authority.

Secondly, the draconian restrictions on advertising in personal injuries matters that were specifically included in Sections 71(2)(h) and 71(2)(i) of the 1954 Act are absent from the Bill as currently drafted.

Apart from that, the definition of advertisement in the Bill is almost identical to that in the 1954 Act as is the definition of inappropriate location.

The omission of specific provision for things such as the categories of information on changes to staff, premises, clients and transactions currently contained in Regulation 5(a) would appear to me to be an anomaly. Apart from that I think one would have to interpret the removal of the restriction on references to specialisms and the removal of the draconian restrictions on personal injuries as a clear change in legislative policy and one would hope that the regulations ultimately made pursuant to the Act will reflect this.

But we will just have to wait and see.

Appendix 2: Data Protection

The other big area of regulation that needs to be considered in marketing, not just by lawyers but by all marketers, is data protection. This tends to be more of an issue for marketing, and more particularly direct marketing, than advertising. Advertising by its nature tends to be broadcast to everyone and no-one in particular (with the exception of one particular online area which I will refer to below.)

Direct marketing can and, as I hope you will have gathered from the main text, should be much more specific. It can involve direct communication to an individual. The information that enables you to engage in this communication is likely to be personal data for the purposes of the Data Protection Acts in that by its nature, the individual is likely to be capable of identification from the data, and therefore how you come by and use that data will be very important from the perspective of compliance with the Acts.

Now, before we go any further, you are a lawyer. You may be far better qualified and able than I to form your own view on the data protection legislation and regulatory regime and you should do so. All I can do here in a text of this nature is provide some general high level guidance points based on my own look at the legislation; but don't take my word for it, an expert on data protection I do not pretend to be.

Data protection is concerned with personal data which means data relating to a living individual who is or can be identified from the data in conjunction with other information that is in, or is likely to come into the possession of the data controller.

The person that holds the data is the data controller and the person about whom the data is held is the data subject.

Sensitive personal data means personal data as to the racial or ethnic origin, the political opinions, religious or philosophical beliefs, trade union membership, physical or mental health, sexual orientation or criminal record of the data subject. Sensitive personal data is subject to far more stringent requirements than personal data generally. However, as sensitive personal data is unlikely to be something that you will be gathering or dealing in for marketing purposes (or at least I don't recommend it) I don't propose to get into the rules governing sensitive personal data here.

Essentially the principles of data protection that are enshrined in legislation are predicated upon consent and at a basic level a data controller must ensure that:

1. Data is obtained and processed fairly and with the consent of the data subject.
2. Data is accurate and complete and where necessary kept up to date.
3. Data is obtained for a specific, explicit and legitimate purpose and not processed in a manner that is inconsistent with that purpose, and is not excessive for that purpose and is not kept for longer than is necessary for that purpose.

4. Data is held securely with appropriate security measures to prevent unauthorised access, alteration, disclosure or deletion of the data.

5. A data subject is informed of the fact that personal data is held and provided with a description of the data and the purposes for which it is held within 21 days of a request in writing.

6. A data subject is to be provided with access to and details of any personal data held (generally in the form of copies of such data) within 40 days of a request in writing.

7. Data is rectified, blocked or erased where there has been a contravention of the Acts within 40 days of a request in writing.

Where personal data is kept solely for the purpose of direct marketing and the data subject requests the data controller in writing not to process the data or to cease processing the data for that purpose, then, where the data is held only for that purpose, the data controller is obliged to erase the data as soon as possible and within 40 days of receipt of the request and not use it for that purpose thereafter.

Where the data is held for direct marketing and other purposes and a request to cease using the data for direct marketing purposes is received, the data controller is obliged to cease using it for direct marketing purposes as soon as possible and within 40 days but also to write to the data subject informing him or her of what other purposes the data continues to be held for.

Where a data controller anticipates that stored personal data will be processed for the purposes of direct marketing, the data controller shall inform the data subject that they may object, by means of a request in writing to the data controller and free of charge, to such processing.

So, the basic rule is that you need the consent of an individual to use their personal data for direct marketing purposes. The Data Protection Commissioner's guide on the subject provides that as a minimum, an individual must be given a right to refuse such use of their personal data both at the time the data is collected (an "opt-out") and, in the case of direct marketing by electronic means, on every subsequent marketing message. The "opt-out" must be free of charge.

You must also make it clear who you are and where you obtained the individual's personal data, where this is not obvious.

These are the basic, high level principles from the Act that apply to the data protection generally. So let's look at a number of specific instances in terms of how data protection principles might apply in those cases:

Direct Mail

Direct mail, or marketing messages sent by post, splits down into two main types in this context: unaddressed mail and mail addressed to a named person.

You're probably most familiar with unaddressed mail from your local supermarkets, food outlets and other retail businesses that send mail drops in a particular locality or geographical area. The mail is not addressed to each householder personally, at most being addressed to the occupant, the resident or the householder in so far as it is addressed at all. Because this type of mail does not identify an individual it generally does not involve the use of personal data. However, where a data controller can identify the occupant, the resident or the householder from the address in conjunction with other data in or likely to come into the data controller's possession, this may involve the processing of personal data and data protection requirements might apply. In other words, data protection can't be gotten around just by addressing mail sent to an address to the occupant when in fact the identity of the person living at that address is actually known by the data controller.

This type of general mail shot is probably not going to be suitable for most legal services but it could have its place subject to Regulation 13 of the Solicitors Advertising Regulations which prohibits a direct unsolicited approach to any person who is not an existing client with a view to being instructed to provide legal services, where this is likely to bring the solicitors' profession into disrepute. However, it could be appropriate in a conveyancing context or if a new local office is opened in a particular area. Generally speaking where the recipients are not targeted by reference to their identity and you do not have any way of knowing their identity, this type of campaign is unlikely to involve data protection considerations.

Then we have direct mail addressed to a named individual. If you are working in the way described throughout this book, you are unlikely to run into problems here; i.e. if you are sending direct mail to someone because they have requested it from you, you are doing so with their consent and at their request and, as long as you make it clear that they can opt out at any time, your use of that person's name and address for marketing purposes will be compliant with data protection principles unless you receive notification from the person to the contrary.

However, where you have the personal data from sources other than a direct request for information – for instance, your existing client database – you have to be more careful.

First off you should ensure, if you do intend using client contact details for subsequent direct marketing purposes, that you obtain the client's consent and provide them with the opportunity to opt out at the outset. The initial letter of engagement seems like an obvious point at which to do this.

But say you have clients from whom you have not obtained express consent but with whom you wish to communicate for marketing purposes. Well, before you can use their personal data for postal marketing, you must tell them that you intend to do so and give them an opportunity to refuse such use. There are many ways in which one might go about this, but the most obvious would seem to be in the initial communication, say with your first newsletter for instance. You might write to the recipient informing them of your intention to send a regular newsletter and informing them of their right not to receive it and providing them with a simple and free means to contact you to be removed from the List if they wish. In fact, I recommend that you provide multiple means to contact you be removed from the List. Similarly each subsequent piece that you send, each issue of your newsletter for instance, should make it clear that the recipient can withdraw their consent to receive further correspondence from you and be removed from the List at any time and at no cost.

Electronic Marketing

The rules governing electronic marketing (phone, fax, text message and email) are primarily set out in Regulation 13 of the ePrivacy Regulations, 2011[5] .

An existing client for the purposes of these Regulations is someone with whom you have had a transaction in the preceding 12 months.

Phone

You may not make a marketing phone call to the phone number of an individual or business other than an existing client who has given consent to the receipt of such calls if they have expressed a preference not to receive calls on the National Directory Database[6].

You may not make a marketing phone call to an individual or business phone number if the person has previously told you that they do not consent to receipt of such calls.

You may not make a marketing call to a mobile phone number unless you have been notified by the person concerned that you have their consent or they have consented generally to such calls on the National Directory Database.

Bear in mind that this aspect of the review is from a data protection perspective. What we are talking about here is cold calling and these are the data protection rules governing it. Cold

---

[5] European Communities (Electronic Communications Networks and Services)(Privacy and Electronic Communications) Regulations 2011.
[6] The National Directory Database (NDD) lists all phone numbers printed in public directories or available through directory enquiries. The NDD contains an opt out register on which phone line subscribers may record their preference not to receive direct marketing calls. Requests to opt out are made via the phone line provider.

calling is intrusive and much more likely to do harm than good to your business and reputation. Also, where non-clients are concerned, Regulation 13 of the Solicitors Advertising Regulations prohibiting direct unsolicited approaches is directly relevant here too.

Email

Email for the purposes of the Regulations includes text messages (SMS), voice messages, image messages, multimedia messages (MMS) and email messages.

The rules relating to email are broken down by three different categories of recipient below. For all email communications, the option to unsubscribe must appear in every email regardless of the nature of the recipient.

A. Individual and Business Clients:

Where you have obtained contact details in the context of the provision of services you may only use those details for direct marketing by email if:

1. The service you are marketing is of a kind similar to that which you provided to the client at the time you obtained their contact details.
2. At the time you collected the details, you gave the client the opportunity to object in an easy manner and without charge, to their use for marketing purposes.
3. Each time you send a marketing email, you give the client the right to object to receipt of further messages.
4. The provision of the service occurred not more than 12 months prior to the sending of the marketing email, or

where applicable, the contact details were used for the sending of a marketing email in that twelve month period.

B. Private Individuals Who Are Not Clients:

If a private individual is not an existing client, you may not send a marketing email to that person unless you have obtained their prior consent and they can withdraw that consent at any time.

Again, keep in mind Regulation 13 of the Solicitors Advertising Regulations in this context also.

C. Businesses (both existing client or non-clients):

You may not send a marketing email to a business if they have notified you that they do not consent to receipt of marketing emails.

Summary

The data protection rules governing the different types of direct marketing communication can be summarised as follows:

	Direct Mail	Email/ Text	Phone to Landline	Fax	Phone to mobile
Individual Client	Opt-Out	Opt-Out	Opt-Out	Opt-Out	Opt-Out
Individual Non-Client	Opt-Out	Opt-In	Opt-In if on NDD otherwise Opt-Out	Opt-In	Opt-In
Business Client and Non-Client	Opt-Out	Opt-Out	Opt-In if on NDD otherwise Opt-Out	Opt-In if on NDD otherwise Opt-Out	Opt-In

Opt-In means you can only market to that person where you have their explicit consent to do so.

Opt-Out means that you can market to that person provided you have previously given them the option not to receive marketing communication from you and they have not availed of this option.

Recommendations

Those are the rules and the bulk of this appendix on data protection is based directly on the Data Protection Commissioner's guide on the subject. But just because you can do some of this stuff, does not mean that you should.

When it comes to postal marketing to existing clients in the context of things like regular newsletters, express consent from all is obviously the best course of action and you should start obtaining that consent now.

However, where you have long-standing relationships with existing clients and have transacted with them recently, then there is a case to be made for an initial communication which explains that you are going to start sending a regular newsletter, for example, and providing them with multiple free means to respond indicating their preference not to be included in any future mailings if that is their wish. Every subsequent newsletter should also include a simple, clear and free means by which to opt out of receipt of any future correspondence.

Aside from that, I recommend you chose opt-in every time. What I meant by this is that even where the Regulations allow you to engage in opt-out communication with existing clients I don't recommend that you attempt this. It annoys people when you email them without their consent. If you do wish to get the ball rolling you might send an email to your clients (in compliance with the Regulations) telling them how to opt-in for future emails if they're interested. You might provide them with some clear benefits for doing so. But don't take it for granted that you can just start emailing them even if strictly speaking you're in compliance with data protection Regulations; that's likely to be completely counterproductive.

Cookies and Re-Marketing

I mentioned at the start of this appendix that these issues are concerned mainly with direct marketing as advertising tends to be more general in nature and is not usually directed at an identifiable individual. However, advertising crosses over the line into this area to some extent when we are talking about online and the use of cookies.

Cookies are snippets of data websites make available to the web browsing software of people visiting those sites. These cookies can speed up the browsing experience on a return visit and can also enable the site to remember the visitor's preferences. Essentially they are a trace of a user's browsing history. And they can be used to target advertising to that user accordingly based on the sites they have visited.

This does not cross over the line to data protection completely as the user's identity is not revealed to anyone as such; rather their browsing history is retained in the browser software. Or at least it can be, however, users can also change their software settings to ensure that these cookies are not retained.

The practical effect of this is that the user can be shown ads online based on their browsing history via a technique called re-marketing.

Regulation 5 of the European Communities (Electronic Communications Networks and Services) (Privacy and Electronic Communications) Regulations 2011 regulates this area and if you use cookies on your website (and you almost certainly do, whether you are aware of it or not) your site needs to obtain consent from users to the use of these cookies. This is usually done by a way of a pop-up on the site that notifies users of the existence of cookies and that by continuing to use the site they will consent to their use. The privacy policy of your website will need also need to inform users if your site uses cookies and if so what purposes they are used for and should generally make the terms upon which users are consenting to this clear.

Index

The Solicitor's Guide

Index

309